Laís
de Oliveira

Hacking
COMMUNITIES

CRACKING THE CODE
TO VIBRANT COMMUNITIES

hackingcommunities.com

Hacking Communities:
Cracking the Code to Vibrant Communities

'Most people who talk about community building want to romanticize it, or worse, they want to make it into a series of actionable "steps" without heart. Laís de Oliveira explains the required actions in amazing detail, but she does it with a sensitivity and a wisdom that can only come from experience (...) Every page gets better and better. If you care about people, read this book'

– Roy H. Williams, Author of the bestselling trilogy: *Wizard of Ads*

'It's both: practical and heartwarming. A book on community building that gives you a feeling like you already belong to something, just by reading it. Lais generously shares her experience as a community builder and lets the reader into "behind the scene", creating this feeling of belonging. Beside rich personal experience told in a raw and authentic way, you can expect to find well-researched insights into community building. If you thought that great communities are born on their own, get ready for actionable know-how on how you can hack a community around your product, company or an idea.'

– Natasha Zolotareva, Journalist, International Media Specialist and Writer at *Entrepreneur.com*

'Required reading for anyone looking to build communities. Part raw accounts from the journey of building communities - from Malaysia to San Francisco - part actionable guide for building communities; this book is a fantastic read. Highly recommended.'

— Arnobio Morelix, Co-Founder & CEO at *Sirius Education*, Author of *Rebooted: An Uncommon Guide to Radical Success and Fairness in the New World of Life, Death, and Tech*

'An accessible and tactical guide to building community. As if Lais, in her work building up Startup Grind and other communities, wasn't enough of a reason to buy the book, her research-based approach to spark and scale communities is so clearly laid out in the book, within the first few pages I was already writing down notes of what I could be doing.'

— Zvi Band, Entrepreneur and Author of *Success Is in Your Sphere: Leverage the Power of Relationships to Achieve Your Business Goals*

Hacking Communities:
Cracking the Code to Vibrant Communities
Author: **Laís de Oliveira**

Visit: **hackingcommunities.com**

Designer: **Daniela Castanheira**
Editor: **Hazel Boydell**
Proofreader: **Michelle Mills Smith**

First Edition, 2020

Published by
Startup Guide World ApS
Borgbjergsvej 1, 2450 Copenhagen
info@startupguide.com

ISBN: 979-858-17745-5-7

Copyright © **Laís de Oliveira**
All rights reserved. Although the authors and publisher have made every effort to ensure that the information in this book is correct, they do not assume and hereby disclaim any liability to any party for any loss, damage, or disruption caused by errors or omissions, whether such errors or omissions result from negligence, accident, or any other cause. No part of this publication may be reproduced, distributed, or transmitted in any form or by any means, including photocopying, recording, or other electronic or mechanical methods, without the prior written permission of the publisher, except in the case of brief quotations embodied in critical reviews and certain other non-commercial uses permitted by copyright law.

For my late grandmother.

Contents

13   FOREWORD

17   AUTHOR'S NOTE

19   INTRODUCTION
         Why Building Communities is Like Coming Home

27   **PART I**

29   CHAPTER 1
         Why Hacking Communities? Why Now?

35   CHAPTER 2
         Eleanor Rigby: From Hymn to Minister of Loneliness

47   CHAPTER 3
         Belonging Is Our Source Code

57   CHAPTER 4
         Belonging Anywhere vs. Fitting In at All Costs

75	CHAPTER 5
	Aligning Directions: The Core Values of Communities

89	CHAPTER 6
	Building Trust: Creating Safe (Vulnerable) Spaces

103	CHAPTER 7
	Sharing (Anything): Cultivating an Abundance Mindset

113	CHAPTER 8
	The Rise of Authenticity: Brands are Conversations

119	CHAPTER 9
	Letting Grow: Humility

127	**PART II**

129	CHAPTER 10
	Defining Community Hacking

137	CHAPTER 11
	Community Life Cycle: Development Stages

143	CHAPTER 12
	From Seed to Sprout: Finding Your Core

159	CHAPTER 13	
	From Sprout to Bud: Building Belonging through Relatable Stories	
169	CHAPTER 14	
	From Bud to Flower: Bringing People Together	
177	CHAPTER 15	
	From Flower to Seed Head: Attract, Engage, Commit	
185	CHAPTER 16	
	Engineering Serendipity: Collision Theory for People	
201	CHAPTER 17	
	From Seed Head to Flying: Closeness Circles	
209	CHAPTER 18	
	Cultivating Dandelions: Let it Grow	
213	FINAL WORDS	
	There's No Place Like Home	
217	ACKNOWLEDGMENTS	
221	THINGS TO READ AND WATCH	
224	ABOUT THE AUTHOR	

AUTHOR'S NOTE

This book will help you develop yourself as a better community leader.

While the title alludes to tips and tricks for community building, its content means to equip emerging leaders with the foundations to build self-sustaining communities. It features personal stories, research studies, and creative metaphors collected during my journey to becoming a community leader.

Disclosure: I especially enjoy crafting scientific metaphors, you'll see. One of my favorites is collision theory applied to serendipity engineering. TL;DR states that increasing the rate of collisions (encounters) raises the possibility of successful reactions (fortuitous connections).

In writing Hacking Communities, I found no shortcut to community building. No quick hacks to going from zero to belonging. As put on page 240 of the Kindle Edition: "I found that you need more than a framework to build a community—you need to step into your journey home, towards your most authentic self." This book is about becoming the leader who enables communities to emerge.

We have been through world-changing events since this book was published (in 2020), from the COVID-19 lockdown to the post-pandemic reality (which we are still figuring out).

In the past two years, we've witnessed the emergence of thousands of virtual communities, followed by accelerated growth in tools and tricks aimed at explaining how to manage them. We've seen the blast of web3 communities into the world (or the metaverse) while investors and corporations, from large to small, tried to catch up (e.g., Facebook changing their name to Meta).

Lastly, we've also seen a growth in the quality and number of community-related executive positions, expanding from Community Managers to Heads and VPs of Community - and Chief Community Officers. Fun fact: I was given the CCO title in late 2016 when FlySpaces acquired my first startup (8Spaces). At the time, I wasn't flattered. I genuinely thought they'd given me any C-title because they had no idea what to make of me - I admit I underestimated my then-CEO being ahead of his time.

Learnings

Since this book was published, I spent two years developing a community-led educational program that welcomed 288 community professionals who held senior leadership positions at companies like Meta, Canva, and Singularity University and plenty of founders and indie community builders (including web3).

As the founding Director of the On Deck Community Builders Fellowship (ODCB), my goal was to carve community as a career path. In doing so, I found multiple ways of being a community professional. Just like Marketing, Business Development, and other business departments, the Community Department has to be seen in its full complexity and broken down into multiple areas, from Strategy, Operations, and Growth (and many in between, including my favorites: Community Design and Architecture).

I jumped from publishing this book to interviewing over a thousand candidates to join that program while developing an educational curriculum for Community Building alongside industry leaders and experts. In this process, I further validated and developed several concepts within this book. Many of these continue to be developed and shared on hackingcommunities.com.

Here I am sharing below some rounded-up concepts and frameworks I've developed since we first published this book, which principles and ideas were present here.

Growth is a consequence of a clear Identity and effective Connectedness.

In Chapter 10, I defined the Three Pillars of Community as Connectedness, Identity, and Growth. The latter is the positive outcome when we, community builders, do a good job defining the first two.

While Growth is the shiny object many companies are after when hiring for a community department, it is but a consequence of a well-defined Identity (which relates to Community Development, Design, and Branding), followed by well-established Connectedness (enabled by Community Architecture and Operations).

The 5 Ps of Community: a better Community Design framework

In the book's very first chapter, I contrasted Traditional Marketing and Community Building to differentiate better and define the latter.

This simple idea evolved into the 5Ps: a simple Community Design framework that helps with teamwork and alignment.

Starting a community departs from identifying, first, its People and their Purpose. Once those are defined, it is crucial to establish the means of interaction between them: what are they committing to do (Participation), how often do they gather (Programming), and where do they stay in touch on an ongoing basis (Platform).

- **People (Who)**: Customer segments, main criteria for identity and belonging.

- **Purpose (Why)**: What they gather for or aim to achieve (individually or collectively).

- **Participation (How)**: Their commitment: what actions they agree to take to deliver value to each other. What defines a key contributor in the context of your community?

- **Programming (What)**: Gatherings, events, and activities that bring them together. How often, where do they meet, and what are they doing during this time?

- **Platform (What)**: How do they stay in touch between gatherings? A platform should be an evergreen space where members can find each other (or resources) at any time needed, either virtual or physical space (a forum, library, or even cafeteria).

If you can't see the 5Ps clearly, it might mean that your members also need clarity. In starting from scratch, I advise always starting with Who and Why before moving into How and What. But in some cases, the What (Programming) helps define the Who - see chapter 15.

User Contribution Journey and Lifecycle: place people as protagonists, not as the audience

I further developed the concepts presented in Chapter 17 (Closeness Circles) into more applicable frameworks: the User Contribution Journey and Lifecycle. The central ideas remain, quoting from the chapter above (in this book): "the more you grow, the more you make space for new roles within your community." The new frameworks help us with implementation within a team context:

1. **User Contribution Journey:** defines a clear path for people to grow within your community (through participation and contribution), from new to top contributors.

2. **User Contribution Lifecycle:** data-driven understanding of the time elapsed from the moment someone joins your community as a new member to when they become a top contributor, and finally to when they "retire" and open space for new top contributors.

These frameworks help you sustainably architect your community by defining 1) how members can actively contribute to delivering your core value proposition and 2) how long they will do that.

The contribution has to be defined by precise, measurable, achievable steps. Referencing Chapter 17 in this book: "It is your responsibility as a community builder to create communication systems that build and maintain trust while providing tools to empower people to help your community grow."

Moving forward

I plan to focus my next book on Community Architecture. I am featuring cases and stories from my own experience but also from community leaders I've been looking up to, mentoring, or advising. Community is an emerging field, and it is constantly evolving. I would love to stay in touch as we develop new understandings that better define the journey, the craft, and the role of community builders.

In the meantime, check hackingcommunities.com for continuous updates.

This note is a quick reminder that Hacking Communities is about developing yourself as a community leader. This book's last chapter: "My personal journey turned this book into a more spiritual than a practical guide to community building."

I wish you an incredible journey of personal discoveries and insights in reading this book.

Best,
Lais de Oliveira
New York, November 22, 2022

FOREWORD

In the early days of building Startup Grind, we interacted with thousands of people around the world: from speakers, to attendees, to community leaders. I personally got on video calls with hundreds of people who wanted to be involved. The main criteria for access to Startup Grind was always a very simple question: does this person share our values? If they did, then we would do anything to get them involved in building with us. If they didn't, then we ran from them as quickly as possible.

Startup Grind's values are simply to give before you take, help others first, and make friends. Few people I have met exemplify those values better than Laís de Oliveira. I first met Laís as she was building the Startup Grind chapter in Buenos Aires in 2012. There, she brought startups and founders together to learn and meet. It quickly became one of our most important groups in Argentina and for our community globally.

We asked Laís to take what she had learned and teach others by joining us full time. In this role, she helped lead expansion from a few dozen cities to hundreds in a few short years. I remember brainstorming with the team one time and she said, "We must figure out how to get Startup Grind in five hundred cities." I burst out laughing. Such an idea was crazy. Were there even five hundred cities big enough for Startup Grind? Could we find enough people who would be interested? But this is the vision and drive of Laís. Today, we have six hundred active chapters hosting fifteen thousand events in over a thousand cities.

I watched in amazement as Laís traveled to Kuala Lumpur and started building yet another community. As a startup founder and the Startup Grind leader for Malaysia, she was equally successful as before. When I visited her chapter in 2016, I was amazed to see hundreds of people following her yet again. Not long after, she moved to San Francisco, where she again started building and leaving a mark. Then, the next time I saw Laís was in Spain, where she was building yet again.

Some people are driven by what they feel is right versus what they are expected to do. Laís is one of those rare people who lead their life by how they think the world should be, and in ways that can help the most people possible around them. This is what makes her the best type of community builder. She is someone who can find common ground with anyone in the world and strive to help bring meaning to them. That's why in almost every continent in the world, she has managed to build community and why her insights on community building are as important as anyone you can learn from on this topic.

Derek Andersen
Co-founder / CEO
Startup Grind / Bevy

December 2020

INTRODUCTION

Why Building Communities is Like Coming Home

"It is good to have an end to journey toward; but it is the journey that matters, in the end."

—ERNEST HEMINGWAY

Community Building: Home

Our individual experiences of home may differ, but most of us can relate to an idealistic idea of home. Home is where your heart is. Home is not a place, but a feeling. There's no place like home.

Home isn't a place, but a symbol. From ancient times, we have cultivated the idea of home as the original place where we feel safe. Our first home is our mother's womb, and our departure from it is our first interaction with pain. This concept is explored in *The Book of Symbols* by the Archive for Research in Archetypal Symbolism, which states:

A house is one embodiment of home; "home is where the heart is," a feeling state of belonging, safety, and contentment. Physically, our earliest home is the maternal womb in which we are gestated, and like the animals who instinctively make their homes in nests, burrows in the earth, the hollows of trees, caves and clefts, many of the first homes of our devising were intimate, encompassing womb like structures. All over the world, cave drawings attest to our primordial presence. Mud huts in parts of Africa are still fashioned in the form of the female torso, with vaginalike slits as doors… To be unhoused is not necessarily to be homeless. On woods, desert, the moon, a ship at the sea, a beloved friend, a particular city, a set of circumstances, is projected "home." These correspond to, or contribute to something within, the experience of a vital center of both fixity and freedom, rest after striving, being fully oneself.

In essence, home is the dream of a place where we are safe. The same book describes home as "the goal of epic odysseys, spiritual quests, and psychic transformations." Home is an internal state of mind that we crave. To find this idealistic place, we often have to leave our existing place of comfort in search of something that might lead us to a lifelong journey.

DEFINE: "AT HOME"

1. RELAXED AND COMFORTABLE : AT EASE
2. IN HARMONY WITH THE SURROUNDINGS
3. ON FAMILIAR GROUND : KNOWLEDGEABLE

We aim to find a place where we belong. That dream of belonging is a dream of home itself—a dream of a place where we are accepted as we are, as our most authentic selves. We crave this place for reasons larger than us—we are wired to belong as a means to survive, which we will explore in Chapter 5.

The concept of home is a key part of building a community. In a nutshell, the path of a community builder is that of someone building a home and welcoming others in to share, own, and help expand it.

Do You Feel at Home Today?

The world has changed tremendously in recent centuries and exponentially in the last 20 years.

Today, we're mobile and connected. Technology has transformed how we interact and expanded our boundaries. We've moved from being defined by our geography or culture to having the freedom to belong anywhere. Access to information has enabled us to find each other online and meet offline. In the 21st century, we are free to belong anywhere and to express ourselves in groundbreaking and authentic ways that were unimaginable in the past. We are free to belong beyond location, nationality, gender, sexual orientation, or ethnicity. The opportunity to build more diverse communities is unprecedented.

Yet, we are the loneliest generation ever. Loneliness is a modern epidemic and it impacts our health in a myriad of ways. We'll explore this topic more in Chapter 4, but for now, I'd like us to consider the idea that if we are allowed to redesign belonging, we must take it. For our own good and for that of our peers and loved ones.

Hacking communities is about building safer spaces for us and others to feel at home in a world threatened by loneliness.

As a community builder, your role is to make others feel at home. This means creating a space where they feel safe to take off their shoes, and where they can be vulnerable and express themselves authentically. Home is where we find true belonging.

To create this space, your first step is to feel at home with yourself. You must be the first to take the courageous step to be vulnerable and express yourself authentically. To do so, you must practice loving yourself first. But this doesn't mean you have to wait until you are fully ready and prepared to build a community—true belonging is not a destination, but a lifelong journey. It is the way home, like Dorothy's journey through the cyclone, Alice's down the rabbit hole and Bilbo's "there and back again."

Our first step is to recognize and cultivate a sense of home. We can do this little by little. Being yourself, or better put, becoming yourself, is a journey, not a destination. Community is about sharing your home with others. It's not about you alone, but about the people you would like to host. First, step into your inner home. Then, be courageous enough to share it with others.

There's No Place Like Home

> *"It's a dangerous business, Frodo, going out your door. You step onto the road, and if you don't keep your feet, there's no knowing where you might be swept off to."*
>
> —BILBO BAGGINS IN *THE LORD OF THE RINGS*, J.R.R. TOLKIEN

From Ulysses's odyssey to Alice's adventures in Wonderland and Dorothy's journey down the yellow brick road, home is the place we crave for, our true north and the destination that defines our path. Let's go deeper into the rabbit hole to make sense of it.

In *The Hero with a Thousand Faces*, Joseph Campbell says the myth is an actual representation of our psychic journeys. What we aim to achieve or gain is a symbol of what we'll look like when we are our most authentic self. We're always walking towards ourselves. We are searching for a state of being that feels peaceful; a mental place where we can take our shoes off and be safe no matter what. Home is the dream place where you can be your most authentic self and know you won't be harmed for doing so. It is a place where you are seen, heard, loved, and cared for.

In his hierarchy of needs, Abraham Maslow put physiological needs, safety, and security first, but he placed love and belonging right after them. Human history shows that there can be no literal safety unless we belong to a group. Just picture yourself hanging out in a savanna around 300,000 years ago, when our species started showing up in the wild. If you had tried to live alone, hunting, gathering, and fighting lions with your bare hands, you probably wouldn't have left any descendants to tell your story. We learned to organize ourselves collectively simply to survive. In Chapter 5, we will dive deeper into the impact of belonging from a social and biological point of view. For now, let's just stick with the idea that safety implies belonging—at least our bodies understand that it does. Thus, being home and feeling safe is connected to being in familiar surroundings where you feel comfortable to exist without thinking, to stay without questioning yourself, and to trust that others around you not only speak your language but also listen to you, taking what you say and do into consideration. They see you; they listen to you.

Building a community is about finding your way home, or rather building a home where you can belong and be your truest self. In building a community, I have found that it is the journey that matters. While we dream of a home as a destination, it is the path we walk that allows us to find ourselves. It is through the people we meet and the obstacles we encounter on the way that we become stronger. It is through the stories we collect that we build our sense of self. Yet, by setting an idea of home as north, we have a sense of direction.

Hacking communities is about belonging anywhere and this pursuit of finding that home is the inner journey to your truest self.

The journey of being a community builder is, first, the journey of getting to know and embracing your truest version. To build a safe space where others feel safe to take their shoes off and open up, one must first be courageous enough to be vulnerable. In her popular TED Talk "The Power of Vulnerability," Brené Brown describes courage as telling "the story of who you are with your whole heart." The word "courage" comes from the Latin term "coraticum," which merges "cor" ("heart") and the suffix "aticum," which implies action. Literally, the word means "a heart act" or "an act from the heart." I call it "acting from your core," which implies being vulnerable.

As a community builder, you must feel at home with yourself, but also recognize that doing so is a lifelong journey. Building a community is part of the way.

The End Defines the Path, but the Path is the End

Keeping it simple: what you aim to achieve defines the steps you take. When planning, you often start from the end goal, the deadline, and then walk back towards your current state to define your first steps.

We usually go through life more organically than this but use a similar method, with our desires guiding the way by defining our choices, from the smallest to the most epic decisions we make.

To share paths, it doesn't mean that our goal needs to be the same. L. Frank Baum explained this well in his book *The Wonderful Wizard of Oz*. I'll take my favorite character, the Cowardly Lion, as an example. He lacks courage—or so he thinks.

As Dorothy, the Lion, and their new friends walk towards Oz, where they expect the Great Wizard to fulfill all their dreams at once, the journey presents challenges. Each obstacle they encounter requires different skills, but every time a challenge requires an act of courage, the Lion steps up to fulfill it, thinking he needs to practice it because he's a coward, which he doesn't like.

Being a coward makes the Lion feel uncomfortable, just like being heartless makes the Tin Man feel bad about himself. All of the traveling friends feel inadequate about lacking something essential. Their insecurities are not about feeling they are "not enough" at the surface, needing to buy the latest car or other luxury to feel better (we will talk about this in later chapters), but about something more fundamental. Baum's characters share a vulnerable journey in which each one seeks to find something they deeply care for. They share inadequacies that define who they are. In other words, they are seeking their understanding of home. While Dorothy's home is a literal home, a physical place in Kansas, it is a symbol of what all of the characters are seeking.

As the Lion makes an effort to be courageous, so the Tin Man is overly concerned with being kind—he is afraid of hurting someone by being heartless—and the Scarecrow tries hard to solve logical problems. Courage, heart, brain, home. We're all in search of that sense of home, of a place where we feel adequate. What's interesting in Baum's story is that the very thing each character feels they are lacking is the one they practice the most along the way. It's this constant practice, the acting upon the inner version of who we believe we are, that allows us to become our most authentic selves. It is the path we walk towards becoming who we are that defines us, and belonging to a community is about walking together.

PART 1
PRINCIPLES

CHAPTER 1

Why Hacking Communities? Why Now?

*"If you want to go quickly, go alone.
If you want to go far, go together."*

—PROVERB

Building Communities is Our Responsibility

The story of this book is one of belonging and loneliness. When loneliness is an epidemic, building communities isn't an option. When loneliness is an epidemic, building communities is imperative. Belonging breeds healthier individuals. It can also bring more loyal customers to your business or a higher sense of safety to a city.

It is our responsibility to redesign communities. Back when we were butt-naked creatures dwelling in caves, belonging wasn't an option but a fundamental aspect of survival. We wouldn't stand a chance against the harsh weather and vicious predators. Communities are the reason we survived, and they can be the reason we thrive.

The world has changed, but our latest update (*Homo sapiens*) dates back thousands of years (both software and hardware). We've grown more mobile and connected. Social media can diversify our networks, helping us expand and maintain connections, but it can also serve as a channel to self-imposed social pressure. The result is generally negative. We show what we want and create a carefully curated display that things are in a certain shape, appealing for more and more likes. If we're having a shitty day, we fall deep in the rabbit hole of "scrolling down " and find hundreds of reasons for self-deprecation. We are never enough, nor are our lives, bodies, or relationships. We keep scrolling. Down and down we go, feeling bad and coping with abuse, whether it's around substances, unhealthy relationships or bad habits. The result is a lack of authenticity, a lack of feeling at home with our bodies. We struggle to fit in. The world has changed, but our bodies are the same. Belonging still matters and loneliness impacts our health.

While such individualism has led to loneliness, technology has also given us the freedom to belong beyond borders. It has opened space for self-expression—we can explore new ways to be. We can relate to others, people much different from the family we were born in and the place we grew up in. Yet, many people don't find a sense of home in big cities. We often live isolated lives while surrounded by people. We distrust our neighbors. While we are free to express ourselves in a city like New York, we don't get the same sense of protection that our ancestors had back in the village. We still need that sense of home.

The way we get together may have changed, but the reason we stay together remains. The same phenomenon that creates a generation of Eleanor Rigbies could also be the birthplace of better communities, where belonging does not depend on nationality, gender, or ethnicity. The world has changed and having the freedom to reinvent communities is an opportunity. We need to reinvent communities by embedding diversity into them. In times of uncertainty, we want relationships, not transactions. We need to reinvent communities.

Most of this book was conceived before the COVID-19 pandemic arrived in 2020. At the time of publication, there is no consistent data to determine the real impact that the related imposed social isolation has had on loneliness and other health issues. What we can affirm is that, although loneliness was a global issue before the pandemic, leveraging tech to reinvent the way we build communities has now become an even more important task.

Definition: Community Building

Let me break this down: there is no such thing as building a community. People already belong together. What a community builder does is to connect them through stories, places, events, or anything else that brings people together. The secret is to bring them together recurrently. Building communities is like building collective relationships. It is about growing familiarity through a cadence of encounters that spark serendipity. Communities develop as people bump into each other more often. It's not about controlling each interaction, but increasing the probability of successful collisions.

The main difference between community building and traditional marketing is that the first talks about relationships the second about transactions.

Traditional Marketing	Community Building
Transactions	Relationships
Product, price, place, promotion	People, purpose, principles, participation
Client, cost, convenience, communication	Core, connections, coherence, cadence
Value from product or service	Value from people around it
Advertisements: One-sided communication, monologues	Conversations in all directions

In Part II, we will dive deeper into concrete examples, including Amazon Web Services (AWS) and its community-driven approach to sales. AWS lets its community speak and make space for it. Its local teams host events all over the world, from meetups to CTO Summits, where local champions take the spotlight and speaking spots. While the AWS team participates in these events, they emphasize providing a space for local experts to share their learnings, fostering a sense of community at the local level. Beneath the surface, they are selling the AWS products and services, that have been powering the endeavors of those local champions.

The essence of a community is people sharing (anything).

We don't share knowledge, resources, or anything with someone if we don't feel like we can trust them. There's no way to trust if you don't have a sense of familiarity, if you are not in a safe space. Community building means creating safe spaces where we feel free to be authentic, willing to help others, and honored to be a part. It is a community builder's role to engineer all the above and make people feel at home with each other.

People need excuses to gather, but what matters is the gathering part. A friend of mine described building communities as "throwing parties with a purpose." A community builder's role is to bring people together enough to create a sense of familiarity over time. The more we meet, the more likely we are to talk, get to know each other, develop trust, and build relationships.

In Chapter 12, we will see that community builders are hosts. They engineer a safe context for people to get together. They connect us through food, coffee, places, online platforms, personal intros, or dinner parties. This book is about building meaningful connections that bring out the best in us.

Key Principles for Community Building

Part I In a Nutshell

Part I outlines the key principles for community building. The following chapters will guide you through ideas that are the *sine qua non* to community building. They will give you the bird's eye view, a perspective of the whole forest. In Part II, we will get down to earth and talk about planting, growing, and navigating through the trees.

This book is intended to be a practical guide to building communities, but while writing it I learned that knowing the framework is not enough. A framework without the wisdom behind it is like a body without a soul, an empty vase. The framework and practical steps that you will find in Part II are like the recipe, while Part I will give you the rationale for everything you need—why you should choose certain ingredients and what they bring to the dish. But don't be tempted to skip to the framework. Understanding the reasons behind it is even more important than knowing it. Let's use my own experience as an example. I knew the framework by heart (since I had created it), but when living in San Francisco I was unable to build communities while I was struggling with loneliness and vulnerability. We will talk about this experience more in Chapter 2.

Communities are where we started. In prehistoric times, belonging to a community meant safety. The world has changed fast, but our bodies are the same. Social isolation still shoots an emergency message to our bodies. Our need for being together, for protection and protecting those we love, remains the same as when it meant survival. We naturally seek ways to belong again. In Chapter 3, we will dive deeper into why belonging is our source code, the impact it has on our bodies, and how we create it.

In Chapter 4, we will examine the difference between true belonging and fitting in. We will discuss the role of authenticity in community building, highlighting the importance of creating safe spaces for people to be vulnerable. We will understand what differentiates a community from a crowd.

In Chapter 5, we will explore the core values of any community. Authenticity, humility and abundance are essential to make sure we create true belonging. I'll give you an overview of each of these values and examine why they matter. Most of us misunderstand belonging and settle with fitting in (pretending to be someone you are not).

We will talk about how to engineer safe spaces in Chapter 6, illustrating it with three stories on how to start and maintain them. We will also go over how to handle cultural change when safety and vulnerability have lost space to false harmony and distrust.

Finally, in Chapters 7 to 9, we will dive deeper into authenticity, humility, and abundance, using stories, examples, and ideas to illustrate the importance of these values.

Throughout this book, I will share stories about building a sense of trust and belonging, which are fundamental to any community. Building community is about creating a series of encounters that can spark successful connections, which I call engineering serendipity. The depth of these encounters doesn't matter. Rather, it's about increasing the probability of successful collisions. Building a community is ongoing work that never ends.

Good communities do not depend on one leader forever. In the best scenario, their founders grow obsolete (examples being Burning Man and Thanksgiving dinners). The community keeps growing organically because its seeds are spread through each participant who shares the same core. Organic growth happens when a core cell replicates itself in a fractal-like system. Even though each fractal may differ in shape and size, it holds a pattern that relates to its initial structure. Similarly, the starter of a community will attract individuals whose cores align with their own. The community we create is a reflection of who we are.

Communities are like dandelion seeds, which will fly and grow through the cracks or wherever they find the right conditions. The goal of a seed is to grow and spread its purpose, shine its light. The goal of a community builder is to be the very first dandelion.

CHAPTER 2

Eleanor Rigby: From Hymn to Minister of Loneliness

"Eleanor Rigby
Died in the church and was buried along with her name
Nobody came"

—"ELEANOR RIGBY," LENNON–MCCARTNEY

The Minister of Health Advises: Loneliness Kills

In 1966, the most popular band of its time—arguably, of all time—released a baroque rock tune that told of "all the lonely people." Its iconic violins still give me goosebumps.

Several fans have attempted to find evidence of Ms. Rigby's existence through the years and a birth certificate featuring the name was sold at auction in 2008, but Paul McCartney stated that "Eleanor Rigby is a totally fictitious character that I made up." The character isn't real, but the theme is, and it's universal. Fifty-two years after the release of "Eleanor Rigby," in 2018, the UK announced a government strategy on loneliness, including the first ever Minister of Loneliness. Worldwide, the lonely are a huge silent community.

The irony is we're not really alone in feeling this way. A study conducted by the British Red Cross in 2018 investigated the extent to which people across the UK suffered from loneliness and social isolation. More than half of respondents feared that no one would notice if something bad happened to them and one in nine people felt like they'd be alone in a crisis without anyone at all to rely on.

The stereotype of a lonely person is someone old, but a study carried by BBC Radio 4's *All in the Mind* in collaboration with the Wellcome Collection found that young people are most likely to experience loneliness, with 40 percent of people aged between sixteen and twenty-four stating that they felt lonely a lot of the time. Twenty-nine percent of respondents between sixty-five and seventy-four felt lonely and twenty-seven percent of those over seventy-five did.

But what does it mean to feel lonely? And why is it a matter worthy of government intervention? In this chapter, we will dive deeper into the impact loneliness has on our bodies, putting a spotlight on our current society and facing the facts: loneliness is (likely) the epidemic of the 21st century.

But first, to illustrate the impact of loneliness, I'll share my own personal story. I experienced extreme loneliness while living in San Francisco, shortly after I had started writing this book. I had written a complete chapter on loneliness and how it impacts our health, yet it took some time to acknowledge that I suffered from the very topic I was writing about.

The Journey of a Lonely Community Builder

"Mrs. Dalloway is always giving parties to cover the silence."

—*MRS. DALLOWAY*, VIRGINIA WOOLF

The deeper I fell into the loneliness hole, the harder it was to get out of it. I rejected most invitations to dinner, drinks, and all sorts of events. When I did attend something, my guard was up. I felt down and was afraid I'd pull the group's energy along with me if I went.

Before I lived in San Francisco, I'd developed a reputation as a community builder. People perceived me as an extrovert and I was often the life of the party. I'd walk out of my apartment in Kuala Lumpur sure that I'd bump into someone. The same thing would happen when visiting Singapore, Bangkok, and Jakarta. Despite these being relatively sizable cities and geographically dispersed, the frequency of meetings were still high. I'd have friends all around. It felt special. Serendipitous. I belonged.

I organized five events a month, from cozy dinners to meetups, hosting entrepreneurs and a wide variety of creative individuals who were paving new ways of doing businesses, living healthier lives, creating better cities, you name it. It felt exciting. People from diverse backgrounds flocked to everything and new ideas flourished.

Psychologists distinguish solitude from loneliness. The first is a state in which one is alone, but doesn't feel lonely. Solitude feels right. I had gotten used to being on my own. I often traveled as a lone wolf, from Kuala Lumpur to Sarawak, Bali to Austin, Bangkok to Tokyo, and more. I took pride in my ability to be whole on my own. I never felt lonely. I had spent entire nights hanging out in bars on my own, oblivious to judgmental looks from strangers. Being alone felt temporary and a choice. Whenever I was alone traveling, I would be questioned (by an astonishing percentage of taxI drivers) about what I was doing there alone, and I never knew what to say. This happened so often that it was funny. I had friends everywhere, so I'd reply, "I got here alone, but I'm not alone."

When I began to feel lonely, it affected a key part of my own identity. Even though I knew that shame is at the core of feeling disconnected from others, I could not get over feeling ashamed of being lonely. Because, *come on*, I had already learned how to belong anywhere, hadn't I? I was able to make friends. Lonely wasn't who I was, was it? Loneliness attacked my own sense of value, of belonging to myself.

Eventually, I left Malaysia and was building a new life in San Francisco. I had old friends there. I had acquaintances and friends I'd made online but not met yet. But I found myself unable to meet them. The times I tried, it wouldn't stick. I'd go to a party, walk around on my own, dance in silence, have some conversations and leave early. I did make a few good friends in the Bay Area, but fewer than I'd made in just six months in Southeast Asia, and 80 percent of the time I felt lonely.

Even though I knew about the impact of loneliness, it took a long time for me to admit to myself that I was, indeed, lonely. Afraid of being a downer and of being rejected because of my heavy, dirty energy, I isolated myself even further. The more I stayed home, the harder it was to get out. If I crossed a friend or an acquaintance on the street, I'd be quick to make up a random commitment so they'd walk on before inviting me anywhere. I believed I would not be welcome if I let them feel my energy. I recognized this feeling—I had felt it back in elementary school. But that was a long time ago. I felt that by this point, I should have learned to overcome it.

On top of everything, this feeling prohibited me from writing this book for a while. I felt like an impostor, a downer writing about abundance-minded communities, a loner talking about community building. I couldn't talk about authenticity. This is how hard loneliness gets us.

Loneliness tells us horror stories about ourselves, about how unwanted we are. How we should be ashamed of showing up. How we will be rejected. What that all means, in the end, is that we don't have a place in the world. We don't have a role. We're worthless. And feeling this way takes us down a slippery road to depression.

I felt like the Cowardly Lion from *The Wonderful Wizard of Oz*. I felt like I was the worst of my kind, not what people expected of me, nor what I expected from myself.

What Loneliness Feels Like—Journal Excerpts

San Francisco, 2019

I never felt this way before.

Feels like a heavy weight on my chest. My heart wrenches, like being pulled in every direction, stretched and crushed at the same time. There's some level of burning to it.

I've googled "things to do," from parties to events from surfing to jewelry making. I considered taking a car or bicycle across town, or to buy last-minute tickets to a party that I just found was happening nearby. Except that I don't feel like going on my own.

Nothing seems to assure me. It hit me stronger with the sunset. It's Saturday night. Then, I considered going to a bar, ordering an old fashioned, rocking it between my fingers while wearing a classic black dress, but I don't feel cool about it. I'd rather have that whiskey straight, in a tea mug, while watching a movie at home. But it's Saturday night a voice inside says. Plus, my body keeps hurting, like urging me to get out. As if staying at home (again) would kill my muscles. I think once again of going to a bar, but the prospect of a few empathizing looks from the bartender or that someone would walk up and talk to me, is terrifying. In fact, I fear and hope that someone will approach me. The idea that it doesn't happen, feels like rejection. The idea that somebody does, feels terrifying. I can no longer recognize myself. On one side, I'd rather not take any risk of engaging in tiresome conversations about myself or the weather with a stranger in a bar. On the other, that contradicts the crushing fear that hits my body, that I'm falling deep inwards.

I was supposed to write about this, and here I am. I dare to google it in search for better words, but there's no better way to put it: I feel alone. I've never felt this before in life and this feeling is no stranger to most of us. It has become my sole companion since I moved to San Francisco. Living in one of the most vibrant cities in the world, feeling the loneliest.

Definition: Loneliness

Loneliness hurts. It's a heart-wrenching feeling. An infinite emptiness pulling in everything that you are, like there's a black hole in your chest. The extreme feeling of disconnection, of being separate. The ultimate heartbreak.

I still can't find the words to describe loneliness, but I'm sure that you will know what I am talking about. Unfortunately, all of us have known loneliness to a certain degree. The closest description I can get for loneliness is a pungent and persistent heartbreak.

> "Loneliness constricts the heart. Loneliness cripples the body and the mind and the soul. Loneliness is unconscious and numb. Loneliness is endless tears for change – any change that will tell you that you are alive. Because loneliness is dying at every moment; loneliness is death."
>
> —FROM "WHAT LONELINESS FEELS LIKE," KOVIE BIAKOLO

In San Francisco, I had a constant fear of rejection, of being abandoned or dismissed. I dreaded feeling this way. I dared to search for what I was feeling, even though I knew, like we search for "flu symptoms" just to confirm we're sick. The answers I found came from Quora responses to the question "What does it feel like to be lonely" and listicles of "Four signs that you're lonely." It felt like the most awkward search in my life. I hoped no one could see my screen.

I found a *HuffPost* article that describes what loneliness feels like, and it struck for its resemblance to my reality. Here are some of the symptoms it listed:

1. Binge-watching the whole season of your favorite series
2. Failing to socialize as you know you should
3. Downtime feels replenishing, while loneliness feels lonely and is linked to anxiety, depression and insomnia
4. You're a Facebook power user

Olivia Laing writes in *The Lonely City* that "when people enter into an experience of loneliness, they trigger what psychologists call hyper-vigilance for social threat.... In this state, which is entered into unknowingly, the individual tends to experience the world in increasingly negative terms, and to both expect and remember instances of rudeness, rejection and abrasion." She adds, "The lonelier a person gets, the less adept they become at navigating social currents."

In the past century, stress has been recognized as a major cause for many chronic diseases. The constant state of being ready to react or feeling under threat introduces large amounts of adrenaline and cortisol into our bodies, holding us for a dangerous amount of time in fight, flight, freeze or fawn mode, which eventually damages our health by weakening the immune system. Loneliness does the same to us. We could simplify it by saying that loneliness induces more stress, while adding an extra layer of insecurity (more cortisol). When we're stressed, everything from driving home to getting a phone call from your boss feels dangerous. For most, it sounds irrational. It feels as if a lion is about to pounce on you from behind a bush at any time. Add loneliness and it feels like you are on your own to face that lion, alone in the savanna.

Your body knows you can't make it on your own. With increasing evidence of its impact on our health, loneliness has become a matter of governmental concern.

In 2017, Susan Pinker, the author of *The Village Effect*, gave a TED Talk titled "The secret to living longer may be your social life," in which she says, "It is a biological imperative to know we belong." Being part of a community was fundamental for our ancestors to survive through time, protecting themselves from harsh winters and hideous beasts. Belonging shoots a "you are safe" message into our bodies through feel-good hormones including oxytocin. Belonging feels safe, safe feels good, and naturally, belonging feels good.

What Loneliness Feels Like — Journal Excerpts

Amsterdam, 2019

My heart rushes as if my life is under life threat, but it is not anxiety.

I'm sitting in the living room of my friends' apartment in Amsterdam trying to get work done, after a day's turmoil has passed. I've been in the eye of the hurricane, and now, it seems that getting out of it will be a trudge through thick walls of dust and dirt. I'm going through it. The hurricane inside me. I can't stop looking at my phone for a hint of a message or a reaction which will temporarily satisfy my neediness.

I try to convince myself I'm not clinging to people or activities who make me feel good, even if temporarily, to satisfy the empty space inside. Yesterday I went out and shopped for 3 pieces of clothing I might not need, but made me feel better. I picture instances where I'll meet and talk to people with these on. They'll like me. I felt guilty for shopping during working hours, even though I've worked 8 hours through the weekend and, yet, couldn't get all my shit done.

I moved to a new city and haven't been amongst close friends for a long time, but I've taken advantage of work-related travels to stay with friends in Amsterdam. I know I've been needing real closeness with people. A space I can be fully vulnerable and relax. A place to be myself.

My friends said I'm overworked, but they don't know how unproductive I've been for the past weeks. No, months.

Back to business, I sit down to work, my brain goes in many other ways that do not help me focus. From bills to pay to emails unread. I check on Instagram for a bit, a picture of a friend pops up, she's with her laptop on a boat, sunset behind, surrounded by a bunch of people - the caption reads something along the lines of "gratitude and feeling #blessed with a life and friends she couldn't have foreseen." I know this feeling; I've been there before. I crave to feel it again... I keep scrolling through more pictures to remind me of my body fat and contradicting relationship advice which could either convince me to stay or leave my complicated romantic relationship. Twenty minutes later, I don't know where my time has gone. I've done nothing, back to work with an even lower percentage of energy than I had before I started scrolling, plus the guilt trip. I keep searching for reasons not to be exactly in the space and time where I find myself today. In every corner, what it seems I'm looking for is a more accurate picture of myself. One that makes me feel closer to home. One I'm at ease opening up with, showing the world. One I don't have to care if it gets 0 or 3,453 likes. One that brings to me the people I can closely relate with. The ones I can trust. The ones I feel at home with. Why does it seem so hard to get?

Making Friends with Loneliness

> *"Hello darkness, my old friend*
> *I've come to talk with you again"*
>
> —"THE SOUND OF SILENCE," SIMON AND GARFUNKEL

What fetched me out of my deep rabbit hole? A series of decisions. I ran off to a nine-day meditation retreat and went back to therapy. And I'm still working on it. Overall, I started acknowledging loneliness, walking towards this feeling, looking at it, embracing it, talking, and learning more about why it existed.

In building familiarity and greeting darkness as an old friend, I figured that it had a substantial role to play in my life if I just embraced it. Loneliness teaches us that belonging matters, that it is real. In the *The Wonderful Wizard of Oz*, feeling inappropriately cowardly is the fuel for the Lion to take small, then larger courageous steps throughout his journey with Dorothy and the others in order to find his true self.

Loneliness is part of the journey that leads us closer to our most authentic selves. Today, feeling lonely gives me a deeper understanding of how real, valuable, and crucial belonging is. In my journey, I have learned to be humble and vulnerable. I have learned to embrace loneliness, to find the path to true belonging. And I know this won't be the last time that I face loneliness. But as we walk, we might as well learn to greet it as an old friend, and listen to the hard truths it has to tell us.

Today, I know that walking through such harsh loneliness in one of the most vibrant cities in the world is an experience I must be grateful for. It was a fundamental lesson to someone who's growing as a community builder. It taught me more about belonging than I could learn from hosting three hundred events a year. It taught me that I still have a lot to learn. It was a humbling experience in which I failed at everything I was supposed to be an expert at: belonging.

In doing so, I learned again that this was a key part of my journey, because the need to build communities is connected to the fear of separation. In Chapter 7, we will dive deeper into it. For now, let's simplify this idea with the understanding that community building would not exist if feeling lonely didn't feel so bad. And we are all prone to loneliness, at any time in our lives.

To some people, loneliness feels groundless. It feels like they've lost everything. I felt exactly like that: in losing my incredible power to belong, I felt lost and fragile. I felt like everything that kept me up was torn down. That feeling allowed me to dive deeper into true belonging, through the path of vulnerability.

Brené Brown says it perfectly in her book *Daring Greatly*: "Vulnerability is the birthplace of love, belonging, joy, courage, empathy, and creativity. It is the source of hope, empathy, accountability, and authenticity. If we want greater clarity in our purpose or deeper and more meaningful spiritual lives, vulnerability is the path."

To summarize, this journey taught me that:

- Loneliness is a human experience. We are all prone to feeling lonely, no matter how wealthy, happily married or charismatic you are. And it's OK. Loneliness is just a passing feeling that reminds you of things you truly care for, like feeling at home with yourself and the others you decide to share with.

- Loneliness can be a gateway to belonging. It is the reason why we care about building communities, just like vulnerability is the path to living a wholesome life.

- While feeling lonely is horrible—and I don't wish it on anyone—it is just another side of the same coin, the dark side of the moon. I'd say that feeling lonely taught me more about belonging than being the life of the party ever did.

Through this experience, by courageously daring to walk towards my most vulnerable side, I was able to sense that some loneliness is necessary for us to nurture real connections.

Loneliness is the reason why, at a point in life, we opt to build more meaningful and less transactional relationships. It is part of our journey towards true belonging, to finding the place where we can swing the door wide open, take off our shoes and sit on the floor, to the place where we will always be welcome.

I wish for you to make it a worthwhile journey as soon as possible.

CHAPTER 3

Belonging Is Our Source Code

"Yeah, it's always better when we're together
Mmm, we're somewhere in between together."

—"BETTER TOGETHER," JACK JOHNSON

Belonging Matters

Why is belonging a matter of life (or death)?

While the world has changed tremendously in recent centuries, our bodies haven't changed in millennia. The earliest fossil evidence of early modern humans appears around 300,000 years ago and there is evidence that the earliest genetic splits among modern people occurred around the same time. We may have office jobs and cell phones, but our biology remains the same. Belonging still feels good—it shoots feel-good hormones into our bodies—and the opposite experience triggers an excess of stress hormones.

Let's explore the origin of communities to understand the roots of belonging. Besides giving us the foundations to the following chapters, this will help us to understand why we must build better communities where more people feel welcome. It is our responsibility.

Hunting and Gathering: The Reason We Survived

Picture us humans in the wild thousands of years ago. Clawless, tiny, naked apes with a random distribution of hair on specific parts of our body (with a prominent tuft on the head). I wonder if we looked harmless and funny to other animals before we started setting stuff on fire, creating tools like stone spears and using complex spoken language to organize ourselves to hunt and gather. If any of these ancient people decided to face harsh winters or ferocious beasts on their own, they likely didn't live long enough to tell their story, and most probably, did not leave any descendants.

As individuals, we don't stand a chance against the fierce powers of nature. Our ancestors knew that. We gathered around the fire together. Came together under the trees and by the water. We shared resources and tasks. Together, we multiplied our strength, and consequently, our potential to thrive. Unlike other animals, humans are not keen on merely surviving: we want to live long and prosper. As put by Yuval Noah HararI in his book *Sapiens: A Brief History of Humankind*, "the real difference between humans and all other animals is not on the individual level; it's on the collective level."

Sharing doesn't come easy, but even back in prehistoric times, it was more than a necessity. We soon realized that the benefits of sharing outweigh the costs. By sharing food and shelter, defining roles, and dividing tasks, we enhanced possibilities for our own development. By having someone specialized in healing herbs, and another in creating better tools and techniques for hunting, we grew further, collectively. Over time, we learned to take care of our children as the future of our community, but also to care for our elders, to trust their wisdom and to honor our ancestors who passed, understanding that they held the knowledge that allowed us to develop over generations. We crafted collective beliefs and created value systems that kept us working together. We started attributing divine and scientific explanations to natural phenomena. Together, we were able to hold space for some to investigate mysteries that would allow us to read the stars, cut through winds and navigate the seas towards new lands while others would document these journeys in epic poetry or film. All of these things were made possible by having everyone involved, including those who held space, kept us safe, or cultivated and prepared us food. Together, we invented and created technology—from the wooden wheel to wifI on airplanes. We do much better as a collective than as individuals. But why? And how?

According to Harari, humans are able to cooperate in much larger numbers through different and complex formats of organization enabled by language and imagination. He calls this flexible cooperation. In his words, "All the huge achievements of humankind throughout history, whether it's building the pyramids or flying to the moon, have been based not on individual abilities, but on this ability to cooperate flexibly in large numbers."

So what does this mean today?

HararI explains that "humans use their language not merely to describe reality, but also to create new realities, fictional realities" and "as long as everybody believes in the same fiction, everybody obeys and follows the same rules, the same norms, the same values." His main example is money—because everybody agrees to believe in its value, we exchange abstract value for actual goods. We are able to imagine fictional realities and communicate them, organizing ourselves to create things that did not exist from spears to airplanes and from wooden to societal structures.

From here, I'd like to use the term "story" over Harari's "fiction." Oftentimes, we craft fictional stories, but stories can also be factual. For example, a myth or parable could use symbolic language to explain, through fiction, why we should not steal from our neighbors. But we could make the same point by telling a real story about someone who, after stealing from their neighbors, was kicked out from their community and did not survive a harsh winter. Whether fictional or not, we tell stories, we craft stories, and we connect through stories.

Back to The Start: The Power of Stories

Myths are a powerful tool to understand our ancestors and communicate with the past, but their symbolic meanings are often misunderstood by new generations. In *The Hero with a Thousand Faces*, Joseph Campbell says, "Every myth is psychologically symbolic. Its narratives and images are to be read, therefore, not literally, but as metaphors." Myths translate pictures from our psyche into worlds. They are metaphors for the language of our subconscious, where deep-hidden feelings and emotions live in the shape of monsters and dragons, luscious gardens and voluptuous goddesses, whatever you fear or please. But we often forget their meaning.

The psychoanalyst and storyteller Clarissa Pinkola Estés retells classic fairy tales and folklore to unveil their ancient meanings. In her book *Women Who Run with the Wolves* she translates symbols and metaphors to modern language, allowing us to understand the core message in each story. She highlights the power of storytelling to personal development, writing that stories are "embedded with instructions which guide us about the complexities of life. Stories enable us to understand the need for and the ways to raise a submerged archetype." In other words, stories give us access to ancient wisdom through symbolic language. Estés explains that "stories engender the excitement, sadness, questions, longings, and understandings that spontaneously bring the archetype."

Oftentimes, the elders and the wise folks in a community were tasked with keeping these stories alive, translating their meaning to newer generations and explaining why it matters. In the current world, when so many languages get lost, we rely on professors, researchers and specialists like Campbell and Estés to explain and remind us of the intended meaning of myth and fairy tales.

Stories remind us of our shared identity. In some cases, a story is only relevant to a specific group of people. In others, the topic is our identity as humans, even if it is written through metaphors and symbolic language belonging to a specific group. Hans Christian Andersen's fairy tale "The Ugly Duckling" is an example of the second form. Estés describes it as a "psychological and spiritual root story." She says that it "contains a truth so fundamental to human development that without integration of this fact, further progression is shaky, and one cannot entirely prosper psychologically until this point is realized."

We will look at the ugly duckling myth in more depth in Chapter 4. For now, what we must understand is that we thrived as a species thanks to stories. They brought us together around the fire, under the tree, by the river and allowed us to pass on the torch of ancient wisdom, teaching us both how to live and how to thrive.

But in today's constantly changing world, these stories that previously brought us together are largely obsolete. Some stories survived through time, but their original meanings got lost. While they lost their relevance, others grew as white noise, relegated to the realm of misinterpretation or converted into dogma. As put by Mark Twain in *The Adventures of Tom Sawyer*, "Often, the less there is to justify a traditional custom, the harder it is to get rid of it."

Dogma implies an absolute truth imposed by some sort of authoritative figure. It could be tradition itself, but also a person or institution. When dogma comes to play, we forget the *why*. Then, we're stuck with a seemingly meaningless tradition. There are usually two ways out of this: one is to re-signify the tradition in a way that makes sense, reminding us of the original purpose so that we can truly relate to it and embody its teachings instead of blindly following dogmatic ideas. Another, is to rebel against it, reinventing tradition. I like to think of what composer Gustav Mahler is widely credited to have said: "Tradition is not the worship of ashes, but the preservation of fire." While the world has changed at an incredibly fast pace, our bodies remain the same. Our need to belong, share and feel safe with each other remains the same as it was hundreds of thousands of years ago.

The early 21st century is the landmark of a world in transition. The turn of the century was a time of change at an incredible pace, with technological advances giving us freedom to belong anywhere, through mobility and connectivity. The experience of living in big cities has given rise to self-expression. We no longer live in small villages, but belonging still matters. Social integration is still a major factor in longevity.

In such times, we don't just have the opportunity but the responsibility to redefine belonging by creating stories that connect us beyond predefined labels. Our identity no longer needs to be defined by our ethnicity, gender, sexual orientation, nationality or social class. It is time we craft new stories that create belonging beyond borders and have diversity at their core. We're not in Kansas anymore.

The Health Benefits of Belonging

Belonging gives us space to excel as a collective. Thanks to our ability to change abstract ideas into reality through language—call it fiction or story telling—we are able to survive longer and organize ourselves around complex roles.

We developed both individual features and collective technologies to stay alive and thrive. Let's take a closer look at some examples. Our "human operating system" (let's call it hOS S, for sapiens) has built-in mechanisms to make us think fast (instinctive) or slow (calculated). Psychologist Daniel Kahneman calls these System 1 and System 2 in his book *Thinking, Fast and Slow*.

We often make fast decisions led by System 1, which represents an impressionist, fast-and-dirty draft of the world that is designed for survival. It makes overly confident, quick judgments which, if scrutinized, would be deemed irrational. Kahneman's System 1 (fast) agrees with our limbic system (or lizard brain) as described by Daniel Goleman in his book *Emotional Intelligence*. Both authors agree that most of what we consider a threat today is our brain's response to the life we lived thousands of years ago. As simplified in a *Huffington Post* article, "when you see your boss's name in your inbox late at night, your body reacts like there's a lion on the loose."

So what's the point? We are no longer in the jungle or on the plains. When you feel under threat, your hOS S activates chemical messengers (neurotransmitters) to get you going. These include adrenaline and cortisol. These hormones play a special role in our daily lives, so let's get to know them.

Adrenaline should advertise like Nike: "Just Do It." It causes us to fight, flee, freeze, or fawn when we encounter a threat. Along with its friend norepinephrine, it makes you take immediate action. A pounding heart, fast breathing, tense muscles and sweating are some indicators that your adrenaline has been activated.

Cortisol is the misunderstood genius. In peaceful times, it controls blood sugar levels, regulates metabolism, helps reduce inflammation, and assists with memory formation. In survival mode, it literally saves your life by maintaining fluid balance and blood pressure, while regulating functions that aren't crucial in a (perceived) life-or-death moment, such as reproductive drive and immunity. But chronically elevated levels of cortisol are harmful. In excess, it suppresses the immune system, increases blood pressure and blood sugar, decreases libido, contributes to obesity, and more.

Stress is essential to survival, but having it all the time can be harmful. When we are lonely, we feel under threat. Due to the ancient wisdom embedded in our body, or simply because of our latest update being thousands of years ago, loneliness feels like we're in constant emergency mode. As a result, we're constantly experiencing cortisol and adrenaline overdose.

John Cacioppo, the father of social neuroscience, affirmed that "the purpose of loneliness is like the purpose of hunger" in a 2017 interview with *The Atlantic*.

"Hunger takes care of your physical body. Loneliness takes care of your social body, which you also need to survive and prosper. We're a social species," he says.

Loneliness is more dangerous than obesity. In fact, some studies reveal that it's about as deadly as smoking.

The Invention of Communities

It feels good to belong. But why?

"Community" is a technology from nearly two million years ago that was built on hOS E, (hOS *erectus*) and that was developed to keep us safe. Our ancient relative *Homo erectus* gathered in communities of fifty to one hundred individuals with some labor division. Maybe there was an uncle Greg (snarl) who was good with hunting tools, and an auntie Ann (grunt) who knew how to discern edible roots from poisonous ones. Her son, cousin Barn, was a renowned sea shell carver. Together, they could feed themselves and their family and protect the group from predators.

We survived because of communities. Belonging to a community activates feel-good hormones in our bodies, which can have positive implications on individual health and a great impact on longevity. Having a community can be better than any diet.

These feel-good hormones include oxytocin. Famous for being the "cuddle hormone," oxytocin is released by human touch. But it can also be activated by eye contact, as long as it lasts thirty to sixty seconds. Oxytocin isn't just about bonding after sex—it's also responsible for trust-building.

To summarize:

    1. Belonging feels safe.

    2. Safe is good.

    3. Belonging is good.

The Fountain of Youth: How to Live Longer

Sorry to break it to you, but overpriced smoothies have little impact on longevity.

Belonging to a community beyond your closest family and friends, however, has a staggering positive impact on longevity, nearly 30 percent over other factors (including vast healthcare) according to data highlighted by Susan Pinker in her book *The Village Effect*. She researched regions in the world where people live longer than average, known as blue zones. Villagrande, in Sardinia, is one such place. Here, both men and women live remarkably longer and there are at least ten times more centenarians per capita than in North America. She researched the local habits, disregarding genetic profile (it only counts for 25 percent of longevity). Needless to say, it included a lot of pasta-eating.

Her research revealed an unexpected pattern to why we live longer: social integration. According to Pinker, "Building in-person interaction bolsters the immune system, sends feel-good hormones surging through the bloodstream and brain and helps us live longer." Regardless of how much cheese, pasta, and wine they consumed, the longevity of people in Villagrande is off the charts. Social structures here play a fundamental role in engineering a sense of community and safety. In Pinker's words, "Like all ancient villages, Villagrande couldn't have survived without this structure, without its walls, without its cathedral, without its village square, because defense and social cohesion defined its design."

This is a summary of Pinker's top ten factors for longevity:

- From 10th to 6th position we have overall quality of life, including clean air, healthcare, and physical exercise.
  The top factor to affect longevity here is physical exercise.

- 5th place: vaccination beats all the above.
  Thank you, Pasteur.

- 4th and 3rd place: quit drinking, quit smoking.

- 2nd place: call mom. Close relationships including ones with your family and best friends have a noticeable impact on how long you live.

- 1st place: social integration. Walking on the streets, feeling safe, knowing your neighbors, and feeling at home in your surroundings. Pinker says that these interactions "are one of the strongest predictors of how long you'll live."

Belonging is a Biological Imperative

So we know that social interaction is good for us. Pinker explains that it generates some feel-good hormones, which may reduce our cortisol levels and positively impact our overall health. In her words, "Building in-person interaction into our cities, into our workplaces, into our agendas bolsters the immune system, sends feel-good hormones surging through the bloodstream and brain and helps us live longer. I call this building your village, and building it and sustaining it is a matter of life and death."

When building communities, it's not about how many people you interact with. It's about making them feel like you understand them and they're important to you. We must go from "I got you" to "I got your back." Building a community shouldn't just be about making your brand stronger, retaining talent, or selling more. It should be about all that plus understanding that you are responsible for making people around you feel better.

CHAPTER 4

Belonging Anywhere vs. Fitting In at All Costs

"This above all: to thine own self be true."

—POLONIUS TO HIS SON, LAERTES,
IN *HAMLET*, WILLIAM SHAKESPEARE

Journeying towards Belonging

Belonging is love-driven but don't get me wrong: this is not a cute, romantic affirmation. Self-love is pure power. Love drives acceptance. Love is essential to becoming a community builder because you need to feel home within yourself to build a home for others.

Note that loving yourself is about the journey; it is more than a static place. You will likely not be done with "loving yourself" while you're alive, but it is important to be on that path because your own journey towards self-love resembles the journey you are providing to the people around you.

As a community builder, you want people to feel they are worthy—that they feel seen, heard, and that their point of view matters. You want them to feel accepted as they are. Even if people within your community talk about being on a journey of personal growth, you want them to know they are (already) enough. If you are building a community around a brand—be it a consumer brand or B2B services—you want people to buy your products or services from a place where it makes their lives (even) better, not because they feel worthless without it.

Self-love allows you to create a space where others love themselves too. This isn't always simple in a world constantly pushing us to be more, where we often feel like we're swimming against the current. This may seem like something new—a result of a late capitalist focus on consumption to satisfy a sense that "you are not enough"—but the constant search for growth, for a place we belong, for a better way is part of our history. From Ulysses to Elon Musk, humans have always felt the need to do something more, to work towards a goal. This need is an important driving force.

In Chapter 2, we read that the need for building communities is connected to the fear of loneliness. In Chapter 3, John Cacioppo told us that "the purpose of loneliness is like the purpose of hunger." But what good can come from fear and hunger?

In this chapter, we will talk about love-driven and fear-driven ways of gathering people. The first approach builds a community. The second builds a cluster of people I nickname the Cool Kids Club. While one is based on belonging, the other is based on fitting in.

The difference between belonging and fitting in is authenticity. When we fear something, we have two options: to make ourselves vulnerable and face it, or to deny and avoid it. We'll talk about the impact of each choice, but before we go into detail, let me say that anything that is not based on belonging is not a true community. You can call it a group of people, a crowd, an agglomeration, but if there's no belonging, there's no community. If it's not love-driven, it's not community. If it's not authentic, it's not community.

The road to authentic connections is vulnerability. In forthcoming chapters, we will dive deeper (and deeper) into why vulnerability matters, and how it manifests itself in practical terms.

Belonging, As Seen on the Screen

Belonging is a hot topic for humanity, from the fairy tale "The Ugly Duckling" to the movie *Mean Girls*. American high school movies are a particularly great example to observe the differences between belonging and fitting in. Most of the time, what we take as belonging is, in fact, fitting in.

Belonging is the real deal. It's what we actually crave—feeling at home with others. Fitting in is what we often settle for when we don't find belonging. We pretend to be something we are not for the sake of being accepted. Belonging is coming home to ourselves through communities, while fitting in means compromising our true selves for fear of rejection.

> *"True belonging is not passive. It's not the belonging that comes with just joining a group. It's not fitting in or pretending or selling out because it's safer. It's a practice that requires us to be vulnerable, get uncomfortable, and learn how to be present with people without sacrificing who we are. We want true belonging, but it takes tremendous courage to knowingly walk into hard moments."*
>
> —*BRAVING THE WILDERNESS*, BRENÉ BROWN

In this chapter, we will also talk about reverse engineering yourself. If belonging is a journey to home, some of us must be brave enough to leave our original homes in order to find our truest self. Not everyone feels safe to be themselves in their original home (whether that's a particular city, a country, or other group) for various reasons. Like the ugly duckling, some of us must journey outside of where we were born or live to find home by connecting with people who bring out our most authentic self. In such a journey, we often fall apart before we get back together. We must let go of our old labels in order to grow. This might mean leaving your comfort zone and daring to be vulnerable with strangers.

In her book *Women Who Run With the Wolves*, Clarissa Pinkola Estés says, "The ugly duckling goes from pillar to post trying to find a place to be at rest.

While the instinct about exactly where to go may not be fully developed, the instinct to rove until one finds what one needs is well intact."

My own journey resembles that of the ugly duckling. Curiosity led me to live across four continents. Born in a small town in the countryside of Brazil, I moved on my own to a bigger city at the age of eighteen under the pretense of studying law at one of the top three universities in the country. But to be honest, it was never about college (by the way, I am a dropout). This journey led me to join a nonprofit that would take me to Mauritius, Argentina and Chile. Later, I'd find a home in Kuala Lumpur, feel lonely in San Francisco and live a short-lived dream in Lisbon before unexpectedly moving back to Brazil ten years after I first crossed the ocean.

The Ugly Duckling Journey:
Building Communities, Not a Cool Kids Club

> *"Because true belonging only happens when we present our authentic, imperfect selves to the world, our sense of belonging can never be greater than our level of self-acceptance."*
>
> —*THE GIFTS OF IMPERFECTION*, BRENÉ BROWN

Owning Who You Are and Creating Safer Spaces for Others to Do the Same

My experience in selecting, leading, and coaching at least two hundred local community leaders across four continents (thanks to AIESEC and Startup Grind) led me to understand that the more insecure you feel about yourself, the more likely you are to create or join a Cool Kids Club, rather than a community. A Cool Kids Club gives you instant gratification, providing you with a badge you can stick anywhere to validate your worth. In contrast, belonging to a community implies that you are worth it, just the way you are.

Our cultures often create the illusion of insufficiency. That is, that we are not enough unless we act and behave a certain way. When your environment causes the fear and scarcity strings to move you, it may be a sign that you must step out of your comfort zone to search for true belonging. As in many characters' journeys, it is time for you to step out the door into exile.

In this brilliant excerpt from *Women Who Run with the Wolves*, Clarissa Pinkola Estés explains what exile means in the context of "The Ugly Duckling" fairy tale:

> When culture narrowly defines what constitutes success or desirable perfection in anything—looks, height, strength, form, acquisitive power, economics, manliness, womanliness, good children, good behavior, religious belief—then corresponding mandates to measure oneself against these criteria are introjected into the psyches of all the members of that culture. So the issues of the exiled wildish woman are usually twofold: inner and personal, and outer and cultural. Let us attend here to the inner issues of the exile, for when one develops adequate strength—not perfect strength, but moderate and serviceable strength—in being oneself and finding what one belongs to, one can then influence the outer community and cultural consciousness in masterful ways. What is moderate strength? It is when the internal mother who mothers you isn't one hundred percent confident about what to do next. Seventy-five percent confident will do nicely. Seventy-five percent is a goodly amount. Remember, we say that a flower is blooming whether it is in half, three-quarters, or full bloom.

Thanks to AIESEC, I directly managed and coached seventy-six young leaders between the ages of eighteen and thirty across Argentina, Chile and Uruguay, and worked with over 350 young leaders from all over the world (literally). Later on, I would interview, select and coach around eighty chapter leaders for Startup Grind across Eastern Europe, Africa and Asia-Pacific regions, in addition to working with over two hundred of them in other ways.

When talking about leadership and management, or identifying the reasons for poor performance in a local AIESEC chapter, leaders frequently pointed fingers at visible outcomes as the biggest problem to deal with: poor sales results, lack of attractiveness to talent, insufficient funds to invest in campaigns that could magically solve it all. But these factors were often the product of a deeper unseen cause. A poorly motivated marketing or sales team was closer, but still far from the actual cause. An intimidated manager who felt afraid to fail and tried not to be too loud about her own opinions was also closer, but also still far from the actual cause. When evaluating how to improve an organization, the goal should be to get to the root of an issue, digging deep to fix it where it starts, not looking at the symptoms, defining a disease based on the superficial, and cutting off the bad ends. To continue the metaphor, I mean not having to take drugs to ease the symptoms of pain and fever, but understanding that the illness is a result of a weakened immune system from stress and poor diet that can be treated with lifestyle changes, precautions, and vitamins.

In the process of interviewing a candidate to open a local Startup Grind chapter, I would check if their actions, stories, and experiences translated our values into reality. Overall, we were looking for abundance-minded people—those who'd aim to make friends, not just contacts, and who would give more than take to the benefit of the whole ecosystem.

I found that the most insecure leaders also tended to be the most authoritarian ones. By authoritarian I mean people who had the following traits:

- Wanting their opinion or ideas to prevail at all costs

- Being defensive at constructive feedback

- Using ambivalent communication, lack of transparency, or holding to information as power

- Playing a two-sided role, conscious or unconsciously making use of "divide and conquer" strategies to keep control over their teams

- Pointing fingers and blaming others for mistakes on their teams

Tyranny, in essence, is a fear-driven type of leadership that not only gets people to act from fear, but part from the very fear it holds in order to rule. It inspires

Cool Kids Club	Community
Fitting in	Belonging
Fear-driven	Love-driven
Must act and be a very specific way	Must be your authentic self
Under pressure	At ease
Leading from fear	Leading from inspiration
Need to validate your worth	Feeling seen, heard, and appreciated
Appearing cool	Feeling cool
Pleasing	Being
Jealous (bullying outsiders)	Curious (welcoming outsiders)
Territorial (fear of losing ground)	Generous (willing to empower others)
Wanting to retain a position	Wanting to grow
Scarcity-minded	Abundance-minded
In it for the win (gaming, transactional)	In it for the people (networking, trust)
Micro-managing	Empowering

fear because it has it. This sounds quite obvious, but you can't inspire a feeling you don't have. We all have many feelings inside, including fear. Choosing who you surround yourself with is like choosing what chords to play. Like a piano, we can resonate in different ways, depending on who is hitting our strings. Making the right choices in who to be with can help you play your best symphony.

If what you have built feels more like a Cool Kids Club, don't be hard on yourself but know that it will always depend on you, meaning that it won't grow if you don't control it. If you are fine with that (or if that is exactly what you wanted) I strongly advise you stop reading this book now. It won't resonate with you. Some leaders, knowingly or unknowingly, create an environment where they are indispensable and consider it a good thing. Whenever you are needed in a vertical or pyramid type of hierarchy, it means you have a Cool Kids Club, not a community. The rest of this book will only make sense to you if you're open to understanding the advantages of letting people own and grow your brand beyond you. If you are curious to learn how to turn a Cool Kids Club into a community, allowing it to grow beyond you, keep reading.

The biggest disadvantage of a Cool Kids Club is that it won't grow unless you force it. Communities, like dandelion seeds, will grow exponentially even if you don't try. It is in their nature to spread organically, growing even through the cracks of the pavement.

In the next chapter, we will dive into building communities, starting by examining the core values that every community needs to embody. In Chapter 6, we will head deeper into what it takes to create safe spaces where people can be their most authentic selves.

The Path to Authenticity: Reverse Engineering Yourself

Becoming your most authentic self comes with a series of small deaths from which you rise reborn from the ashes, like a phoenix. Poetic? Let's get down to examples.

Sometimes you have to deconstruct predefined versions of yourself to find your truest version. It is easy to get lost in the process (that is, to have an identity crisis) and it might hurt, but as soon as you've gone through the motions of breaking up with your own labels, grieving and, finally, reinventing yourself, you will know it was necessary.

These small deaths can be rather practical, or more attached to aspects of your personality that feel hard to part with. I have a personal story to illustrate that. I thought I could speak decent Spanish when I moved to Argentina in 2010, but I soon found out that I didn't. I could not engage in natural conversations, and I couldn't make (nor catch) jokes. That I lacked the language skills was evident and concrete enough for me to acknowledge it. There was no way around it and denying wasn't possible, so I had to address it.

In Brazil, I had defined myself as a group joker. I was the first with a sharp comeback, taking my native Portuguese and years of contextual humour for granted. I thought of myself an extrovert until my lack of fluency in Spanish inhibited me from communicating at the required pace for natural interactions with my Porteño friends—most of whom had known each other since childhood. This, plus not having the extended slang vocabulary, pushed me deeper down into the introvert hole. Rather than being the joker, most of the time I sat around listening and nodding.

Before Argentina, I had lived in Mauritius and did not have the language barrier issue there. My guess is that in Mauritius I was in such a blend of cultures that no one felt 100 percent comfortable to throw jokes around, yet we found new ways to understand each other. Diversity was embedded in my friend group there. My closest connections there were with people from a colorful range of places including Mauritius, Kenya, Tanzania, India, China, Austria, and Pakistan.

With that experience behind me, I thought I'd blend in easily in Argentina. But Buenos Aires felt harsh. Since then, I've come to find that several large cities (including São Paulo, Rio de Janeiro, and Paris) share certain provincial traits: native citizens tend to hang out in rather closed groups, while outsiders befriend other outsiders.

Back to Buenos Aires. I had been dating a Porteño and it took time for me to feel at home with his group of friends. It was hard to belong without trying to fit in. In other words, it was hard to make myself one of them without forcing it, even though they seemed welcoming.

There was a time, at a dinner party, when I had been hopping seats, trying to engage in any conversation, until they all gathered around someone's phone to listen to a funny audio clip. It was evidently hilarious—some of them even had tears in their eyes from laughing. But I didn't get the joke. I started laughing hard because it seemed like the least I could do. Soon, instead of looking at the phone, they were looking at me and still laughing. They knew I didn't understand. I knew I didn't understand. They were laughing at the joke and I was laughing because they were laughing. Eventually, they were laughing at me and I was laughing because I was nervous.

Maybe I should have asked someone to explain the joke. But back then I had less experience with vulnerability as a means to truly connect with others. At the time, I felt too much like an ugly duckling already. I was ashamed of reinforcing the fact that I really didn't get the joke by asking why it was funny. Today, I'd do it differently. I'd ask them to explain the joke without letting my shame get in the way.

This story is just one of many that illustrates how I did a poor job at "fitting in" amongst Porteños. Episodes like these pushed me to learn Argentine slang, and to do it fast. It had become a necessity, not just a means of communication but a way to belong authentically. To make sure they would laugh with me, not at me. This harmless episode was traumatic at the time, but it taught me that "fitting in" was not a good road. By faking a laugh, I got a worse outcome than just admitting I didn't get the joke. This is what fitting in generally looks like: inauthentic.

According to therapist and teacher Nora Alwah we lie to protect ourselves or something we hold dear. In a speech titled "Embodying Our Full Selves with Mindful Lying," she posits that we lie to protect our connection with others, because "the need for acceptance is stronger than the need to be honest." As we've seen, belonging is coded in our bodies as fundamental to survival. Alwah also explains that "lying is a survival mechanism. It doesn't matter if it is a real threat. Our nervous system doesn't differentiate between real and perceived threat."

As a queer cis-woman of color with European-African roots, Nora Alwah understands both through her practice and personal experience that "being honest is a tremendous privilege... Anyone with a marginalized background knows the pain of not being able to share your whole truth." But she says that we can learn a lot by looking at the times we are not able to be honest with ourselves and with others, telling us that "lies are these tiny little messengers, and they just come to remind us that we experience pain.... We choose deception, including self-deception, over integrity. Honesty is so incredibly uncomfortable."

For most of us, it's not as simple as simply waking up one morning and sharing our truest selves with the world. As Brené Brown says, "You share with people who've earned the right to hear your story." We need safe spaces in order to be vulnerable and show the world our truest versions. This is why we need communities, where belonging is *sine qua non*.

Fitting in is a way of hiding your vulnerabilities, caused by feeling threatened or afraid of rejection. Fitting in is a fear-driven mechanism where we are willing to compromise who we truly are in order to feel accepted by others. In *The Gifts of Imperfection*, Brené Brown says "Belonging is the innate human desire to be part of something larger than us. Because this yearning is so primal, we often try to acquire it by fitting in and by seeking approval, which are not only hollow substitutes for belonging, but often barriers to it."

True belonging is based in vulnerability, which makes space for you to express yourself with authenticity. Vulnerability implies trust, and it is love-driven. While fitting in argues that you must be part of a group, no matter what, belonging rests in the comprehension that being part of anything is only worth it if you feel at home with it.

I failed at fitting in, but it turned out to be the best thing. From this failure, I dared to find my path to belonging through trust, vulnerability, and authenticity.

Humor: A Tool for Bonding or for Bullying?

Finding something funny is a human thing. But humor is extremely cultural.

Essentially, a joke is a relatable story that describes something ordinary but ends with something unexpected. It brings an extraordinary element that surprises the listener. In a nutshell, finding something funny relies on interpreting reality in similar ways, having long shared similar experiences that define what we expect of something at a collective level. What makes it laughable is the unexpected outcome.

Knowing that humor is based in shared experiences leads us to understanding the power of inside jokes both as a means of inclusion and exclusion. Humor is cultural. On a large scale, you can think of a national, or international group that shares similar jokes based on a similar interpretation of the world and their surroundings. But culture can also be created on smaller levels.

You probably had inside jokes with your closest friends at school. Perhaps you spent a lot of time sharing ideas and feelings about certain topics, teachers or people in your class. Similarly, you would probably laugh if a colleague cracked a joke about your shared boss, or if your boss cracked a joke about a team behavior that you can relate to. We make fun of things with the people we trust will understand us.

Inside Humor (yes, capitalized) can be positive or negative to community building.For instance, making fun of your boss or teammates can be good, as long as they are laughing with you. The key question, then, is which people would you like to include in your community? Are they all listening to the joke? And if they are, are they laughing with you? Any joke that includes whispering behind someone's back or causing them to blush and hide their face, offended or embarrassed, is a joke that excludes that person. Anyone who is not hearing, not understanding or not laughing (genuinely and wholeheartedly) is excluded.

Humor can be a good way to integrate with others. By telling a joke that others get, you immediately connect with them, up to a certain level. A shared joke communicates that you understand each other. It becomes even better when we can laugh about ourselves. Either you are making fun of yourself, or of the group as a whole (talking about its traits that you also share). This implies vulnerability. It shows that you and the group have the courage to look at your own flaws and laugh about it lightheartedly, while knowing that it might be an issue you should discuss on a serious note next Monday. Making fun of awkward situations may be a way to make them light. It can be inclusive if the joke aims to include everyone involved in laughing about a recognizable situation. For instance, a lighthearted joke about a poor aspect of your company culture may help bring attention to an issue everyone needs to deal with in a playful way. I believe that humor is, overall, a positive thing in building communities.

Unfortunately, I see it often being used in the Cool Kids Club way. That is, when we laugh at others, not with them. Laughing at others is the essence of bullying. Making fun of the way others dress, walk, or talk, just because it is different from the way we do, is like finding others' habits unacceptable just because we don't understand them. In essence, we are afraid of what we don't understand. While we agree that bullying is bad, we still tend to judge what we don't know or understand. You may have accidentally judged someone. Being confused about someone's behavior or ways of thinking is normal. The issue is what you do from there. The danger lies in thinking or assuming that whatever we interpret about a person is right. The first tip on how not to be a bully is to admit that you may be wrong. Or weird. Maybe you are the crazy one.

Throwing out an inside joke intentionally, knowing that one or more people within the circle will not get it or will get offended by it, is a form of bullying. Humor can be a great tool in building communities. Just make sure that as you use it in a respectful way and that everyone in your group is laughing with you.

Belonging Fast: Be the Foreigner

Let go of who (you think) you are

> *"If you travel far enough, you'll eventually meet yourself."*
>
> —JOSEPH CAMPBELL

Getting out of your original home is a great way to become more authentic. It doesn't matter if you cross an ocean, move to a new city, change schools, or try a different cafe to hang out and meet new people. What matters most is that you get out of the place where you identify with a certain brand or role. Run just far enough from your village, choose a different landscape, find a place where people do not speak your language nor share the same background. Talk to people who, at first, would not get your jokes. You don't need to fly hundreds of miles to have this experience. Some of us can experience having a cultural abyss within our own neighborhoods.

Traveling alone for several years taught me a lot about safety. I am physically unthreatening, with thin wrists and below-average height. The way I helped myself feel safe in different places was by connecting with people. When you are the foreigner, you learn to listen and observe. When everything looks different between you and others, you learn to scan fast for anything you share in common. You learn to find the reasons you belong there, why you can be one of them.

The first thing you find, when positively looking for similarities, is that you and the people around you most likely both stand on two legs and probably have a rather hairless body compared to other animals, except for that tuft at the top of your head. You probably both have a pair of eyes, a nose, and a mouth. You don't need to dig deeper to find you both feel hungry and thirsty frequently, and both of you probably enjoy having a roof over your head and people to share it. If not the roof, you probably enjoy sharing at least your food and drink with people you care for. And most importantly, you both have a heart. You're both human. I know this sounds obvious and perhaps borderline cliché, but unfortunately we tend to forget the basics. I have no more creative way to say that, as humans, we share a lot, before even considering where we came from, the color of our skin, or what causes or football team we stand for.

When did we learn to fear each other?

In practical terms, I like to think of food as the first element in bringing us together. Sharing food is a bonding experience that gives us time to have conversations that could bring us closer. In fact, it's not about the food really, but the conversations around the table. We'll dive into this more in Chapter 17. For now, let's consider a quote by William Butler Yeats: "There are no strangers here; only friends you haven't yet met."

To belong fast, you first must let go of everything that labels you as anything in the place where you came from, because it might mean nothing where you're going. From my first experience living abroad, I learned to follow these practical steps:

1. Accept you are the foreigner. The crazy one. Learn to listen and observe.

2. Identify ways to communicate (even if you don't speak the same language) and start by giving first. Make friends.

3. Always assume that people are willing to welcome you as one of them.

Being from Brazil, where distrust is (unfortunately) a rule, I am aware that the world has taught us not to trust each other, just in case. I am not telling you to get in a cab with somebody you just met at a bar. Please, don't. What I am saying is to open up to the possibility of connecting with people to find out they could be kind and caring.

Acting curious at cultural differences is (maybe) something we could not afford to do in the past, when anything foreign could be a potential threat to the survival of your whole tribe. It is time we recalculate that belief.

At many points in history openness and collaboration has led to progress rather than extermination. More often than not, learning something new, like someone else's language and technologies, would lead to accelerated development. Italy only flourished during the Renaissance because it was the doorway between Western and Eastern civilizations. Thanks to this confluence of both minds and spices blending together, this was a time of great advances in art, science, and architecture that inspired a whole new world. Silicon Valley only became the birthplace of startup ecosystems through people being open and embracing each other's ideas. We will examine this more in Chapter 7, when we talk about having an abundance mindset.

You Don't Need to Cross an Ocean

Look at people around you as if it were the first time.

In order to start a new relationship, you must open yourself up to getting to know the new person you're interested in, their likes and dislikes. To get to know them, you might even be open to trying new things, like that Japanese restaurant you never went to because you don't like seafood. In getting to know the other person, you might also find out new things about yourself. Maybe you really like that restaurant and it becomes the first of an Asian food trail.

New people can bring out previously unknown aspects of you. It does not mean that they are changing who you are, only that they are bringing up the things you already had in you, but were hidden deep inside or fast asleep. Whatever resonates with you indicates something you have inside.

We are like pianos made of flesh and bone. We have a collection of diverse chords inside, but can live a life without some ever being played. Sometimes we meet people who hit us right on those untouched chords, and the sound can either thrill us or scare us. We might be moved by these people for reasons unknown, attracted by a rational excuse or by that touch of *je ne sais quoI* that we may call their energy, their vibe or something else. What brings us together is often an excuse. What binds us together is what matters. "We met at a rock concert" or "I found myself at this electro rave and there she was, looking bored, sipping beer in a corner and wearing a Fleetwood Mac shirt" have a similar "what," but the "why" is deeper inside. Liking the same kind of music can tell us more about each other than the musical taste itself. Loving jazz or hip hop is beyond enjoying a good beat. It's a statement.

Building communities is like building collective relationships. You must follow a similar process as when you're making new friends or falling in love with someone new. This process might challenge you to see parts of you that maybe you didn't know about, for good or bad.

Building communities includes:

- Being curious. It's not about you. It's about them. You want to know everything about their tastes: what they like, who they are, where they come from. You want to share about yourself, but first you want to listen and learn the most you can, to share what really matters.

- Being open to change. Try that new type of food, attend a music concert you otherwise wouldn't, watch that movie you'd never pick by yourself. In the process of listening and daring to do new things, you are also getting to know yourself.

- Adding value first. In learning what the other person likes, offer experiences they might enjoy. Create spaces where you can be your most authentic self, so you also open space for them to be vulnerable and feel safe around them. Build a home for all of you.

You don't need to cross an ocean to be curious about people.

To build communities within a neighborhood, start by erasing everything you think you know about yourself, as well as everything you think you know about your neighbors. Break predefined labels that create an illusion of knowing each other. Start anew and see what happens.

Getting into a new relationship with someone, from the moment of attraction to the moment you commit to each other as friends, partners, or anything else, means daring to find new versions of yourself. It means walking together from "what" brings you together to "why" you stay together. We will dive deeper into the "what," "how," and "why" we stay together when talking about the building relationships funnel in Chapter 16.

A relationship is only true while the people in it are interacting with each other, having regular conversations and listening to each other, sharing time, space, food, or experiences, daring to grow together and never, ever taking commitment for granted. Commitment is a belief shared by two or more people. Underneath it, what actually gets them to stick together is genuine care, translated into continued interactions, conversations, and mutual exchanges.

At its core, what really matters in community building is building relationships based on authenticity, where everyone feels like giving their best and caring for each other.

CHAPTER 5

Aligning Directions: The Core Values of Communities

"You are only free when you realize you belong no place—you belong every place—no place at all. The price is high. The reward is great."

—MAYA ANGELOU

Fundamental Values: Authenticity, Humility, and Abundance

What makes a community?

The word "community" is derived from the Latin *communitatem*. Reportedly, this originally meant "fellowship, community of relations or feelings" but in medieval Latin came to mean "a society, a division of people." Today, we understand community to mean a unified body of individuals, whether that's people with common interests, people with a shared background, or a group of people living in a particular area. I'm not a fan of definitions, since they are often limiting. Communities are rather complex. The important part is that the word "common" is at the core of community. I understand communities as people sharing (anything) consistently, regardless of their location, nationality, gender, ethnicity, or sexual orientation.

Let's break it down:

- People: implies a collective

- Sharing (anything): is having something in common with others (space, ideas, food, needs, ideals). It implies giving, dividing, or being together around something.

- Consistently: means it is a continuous, repeated encounter. This is like building a relationship.

When building communities, we often highlight "what" brings us together: food, fire, shelter. In reality, what connects us doesn't matter as much as why we stay together.

Hugh Mason, co-founder and CEO of JFDI Asia, says that "community building is like the turkey in the Thanksgiving dinner: people get together to eat the turkey, but what matters are the conversations around the table." A renowned community builder and a good friend of mine, Hugh co-founded JFDI as one of the first startup accelerators in Singapore. It played a key role as a lighthouse and cohesion point for the Southeast Asian startup community. Hugh and his co-founder did not play a centralizing role in it, but created a space for people to get together.

In this chapter, we will talk about the three core values that make a community. From the Latin cor, the word "*core*" refers both to heart and (more recently) to seed. Without core values, a gathering could gravitate towards becoming a crowd, or worse, a Cool Kids Club. At every gathering, people are sharing space, ideas, and maybe other things like food. But as we have discussed, anything that is not based on belonging is not a community. Community implies continuous encounters built on safe spaces, which enable trust to grow.

Let's dive deeper.

The Core Values of Communities

In the long term, why we gather matters more than what brings us together. Another key factor is how we stay together.

Communities are about sharing (anything). The why means walking in the same direction, setting the tone for the path we walk towards: the how. Sharing values is like defining how we interact. Our *modus operandI* is defined by our core.

Hugh Mason told me that if you had asked him "Who are you?" ten years ago, he would have said "a storyteller." Today, he calls himself a community builder. As discussed in Chapter 3, building communities is about creating stories that connect people. In ancient times, tribal chiefs or village elders were storytellers at large. A community implies a shared story. According to Yuval Noah Harari, "as long as everybody believes in the same fiction, everybody obeys and follows the same rules, the same norms, the same values."

Simon Sinek, the creator of the Golden Circle, says the same thing in a different way: "The goal is not just to sell to people who need what you have; the goal is to sell to people who believe what you believe."

We tell stories to align behaviors.

From ancient times, we have told stories that translate our core values into metaphors. Today, we tell stories in the shape of company manifestos or paintings on the walls featuring a mission and vision. But creating a beautiful company manifesto isn't enough. You need to reinforce it through daily action that demonstrates you are, authentically, what you say.

I have adapted Simon Sinek's Golden Circle framework to craft stories that build great communities. We will explore it more in Part II, where we take a handbook approach for community building.

In a nutshell, authenticity is good for business. It's not about convincing people to believe what you believe, but about communicating your values and trusting that people with similar beliefs will come together. Having shared values is a key part of belonging to a community. But which values are we talking about?

People within a Cool Kids Club can also share values, but these values often come from a scarcity-driven belief. They might think that they are not enough, feeling the oppressive need to be something specific to fit in. A community implies that people feel at home while being their most authentic selves.

There may also be groups where people believe that someone else's success is their ruin, that life is a zero-sum game where someone else winning means they lose.

In this scenario, people will do everything in their power to defeat others, to cheat, to take care of themselves first because no one else cares. That might sound familiar, especially for those who grew up in scarce environments. From growing up in an emerging economy, I find this to be an unfortunate pattern. In a context where corruption is expected, there is an institutionalized lack of trust that pits individuals against each other.

We need to reinforce the creation of safe spaces where people feel at ease being authentic. The more at home people feel, the more they tend to wish others well, knowing that when everyone wins, they also win. When I do not have to fight for myself, I am more willing to give first.

While different communities can have a broader set of different values, these core values are intrinsic to every community. Regardless of what people gather around, trust and sharing needs to be involved. We only call it community when it's based on true belonging. I call this concept core values because all other values emerge from it like seeds. Without it, there is no community.

I spent a long time studying communities. From nonprofits to companies, activists to entrepreneurial communities. I read their manifestos and listened to their leaders talk about what made their business work. I researched and interviewed community builders from the fastest growing startup ecosystems: Singapore to Stockholm, São Paulo to Silicon Valley. I tried to decode their value systems, drilling down to the very core. I went back to ancient wisdom. I read stories, from Clarissa Pinkola Estés to John Cacioppo.

Then I had my *aha!* moment while writing this book. After drawing a bunch of cause-and-effect mind maps, drafting correlations, playing with Post-it notes, it became obvious. The core values of community are the AHA: Authenticity, Humility, and Abundance.

Why this specific trio? Because everything else is either an action or a consequence of these values.

By action, I mean creating safe spaces where people can express vulnerability. Or building familiarity through repetition to enhance trust. Having a culture of giving where people feel like the rising tide lifts all boats. Building ownership and empowering people to speak on behalf of the community, etc.

By consequence, I mean the critical evidence or key characteristics that allow us to recognize a community as such: identity, connectedness, and growth.

Now, let's understand the AHA.

Why Authenticity?

> *"Authenticity is a collection of choices that we have to make every day. It's about the choice to show up and be real. The choice to be honest. The choice to let our true selves be seen."*
>
> —*THE GIFTS OF IMPERFECTION*, BRENÉ BROWN

There is no community if we are deceiving ourselves and others to fit in. How many of us start projects, go places, attend parties, buy things and each time become more like someone else, until we no longer recognize ourselves?

And how many of us feel threatened to reveal our true self and be seen? The threat may not be real, but the perception of it is. Bringing back Nora Alwah, "Anyone with a marginalized background knows the pain of not being able to share your whole truth." True belonging can only find its way through authenticity.

Authenticity builds relationships, not transactions. One of Startup Grind's core values reads: "make friends, not contacts." Authenticity is what makes us feel like home. Authenticity is the gateway to true belonging.

In *Braving the Wilderness*, Brené Brown says, "Fitting in is about assessing a situation and becoming who you need to be accepted. Belonging, on the other hand, doesn't require us to change who we are; it requires us to be who we are."

Our first step is to recognize and cultivate a sense of home. Being yourself—or, better put, becoming yourself—is a journey, not a destination. It is the way home, like Dorothy getting caught in a tornado, like Alice falling down the rabbit hole, like Bilbo trekking to the Lonely Mountain. It is a journey "there and back again."

Then, when you're on your way to becoming yourself, it is about sharing your home with others. It's not about you being alone, but about the people you would like to host. By making people feel at home and safe, you cultivate their loyalty and help them on their own journeys. You are doing good in creating spaces (whether virtual or physical) where they can belong in a world with the ever-present threat of loneliness.

> *"I'm not scared to be seen*
> *I make no apologies, this is me."*
>
> —"THIS IS ME," BENJ PASEK AND JUSTIN PAUL

From a practical perspective, authenticity is about energy efficiency. When you're authentic, you pump fuel straight from the heart. You're less sensitive to people's thinking and more connected to what drives you. Reinforcing authenticity helps others to resonate with you. It increases your power to attract and connect with others who share the same beliefs and who could walk further with you. Acting from your core saves money, time, and generates more energy that you can spend doing more of what you're good at.

AUTHENTICITY = EFFICIENCY

When you build a brand from a strong core, everything you say and does resembles you.

Why Humility?

> *"Always remember that you are unique. Just like everyone else."*
>
> —MARGARET MEAD

The concept of humility blends well with the very concept of belonging: to feel part of.

Humility emerges from self-love. It comes from feeling at home, from feeling seen. Recalling what we discussed in Chapter 4, self-love is pure power and love drives acceptance.

Humility comes with quiet confidence. It means truly loving yourself, knowing you are enough. When you belong, you do not need to prove yourself, make a point, compete, or show off. You need no spotlight unless being in it is part of your truest self.

Humility is like saying, "I'm glad to be a part of this. I am humbled to belong. I care about the collective, as I am part of it. I care that our mission is accomplished, regardless of whether it carries my name or not. I care about the results over recognition. I don't need to validate myself here. I am enough. I am seen, so I need no spotlight. No competition. I am part of the whole." Perhaps this sounds too much like a hippie positive affirmation for you, but I just hope you continue reading to the end of this book and give the idea some consideration.

Humility yields confidence.

Our society overestimates the value of standing out from the crowd. Standing out can be good. At times, a revolutionary act paves new ways for others to be different too. But some of us might have gotten addicted to the idea of being special. We normalize the competition. When "you are not like other girls/guys" becomes a compliment, it implies that you must compare yourself to others to qualify yourself. Competition can be a good thing—it inspires us to look around outside of ourselves, get inspired, to learn from others or level up. But when it is the core driver for your actions, you lose authenticity.

Through mobility and connectivity, technology enables us to belong anywhere. It can expand our boundaries towards new, colorful, beautiful ways to belong. But it can also create another type of abyss. Many problems in the world are due to excessive individualism. Too much focus on the individual means competition, power fights, and, at its worst, separation, which is the gateway to loneliness. Feeling separate from the rest and having an "us and them" mindset has practical risks. We live in a world where divide and conquer is an actual power technique applied on multiple levels. Countrywide, it helps win elections. At a corporate level, it allows for authoritarian (aka insecure) leaders to hold on to power, regardless of whether they are actually good for results.

But as a company leader, why should you care about humility? What is the practical benefit of thinking as a collective, rather than as an individual?

Patrick Lencioni, a renowned author on corporate leadership, created a framework demonstrating that high-performance teams have members focusing on the common good. They feel responsible for collective goals and vision. This sense of ownership comes from truly buying into each decision, which comes from communicating authentically and from sharing a safe space.

He presents this model for team management in his book *The Five Dysfunctions of a Team*. LencionI explains that feeling safe to express yourself authentically gives you a sense that you are part of something. The more you belong, the more you care. When you belong, you feel part of something larger than yourself and are more likely to be humble.

Think of snowflakes. Each has a unique design. But a single snowflake makes no snow. Humility tells us to find peace in belonging to something bigger. It tells you that you are special—just like everyone else. Being humble allows you to let the community grow, knowing it is larger than you.

> "You are not your job, you're not how much money you have in the bank. You are not the car you drive. You're not the contents of your wallet. You are not your fucking khakis. You are all-singing, all-dancing crap of the world."
>
> —*FIGHT CLUB*, CHUCK PALAHNIUK

Why Abundance?

Abundance is a state of mind where you believe that the rising tide lifts all boats. It implies trusting that someone else's success is good for everyone, including yourself. It means trusting amazing things are about to happen and rejoicing in other people's joy. It is knowing that we thrive by being part of a collective and that we rise by lifting others. It is recognizing that we don't need to fight for the last slice of pizza, but instead, can make more pizza together.

Does this sound too idealistic? Let's get down to earth.

Creating abundance facilitates sharing, meaning the flow of knowledge and resources. Above all, it means optimization. We gain more when we share. But more often than not, we are raised with the idea that by sharing, by giving first, we might be tricked, fall behind, and ultimately lose.

The best example of why abundance matters are at fast-growing startup ecosystems, especially during the first generations of founders, when startups were still unprecedented.

The Economic Impact of Abundance

In 2012, I joined NXTP Labs, an Argentinian organization that was one of the first startup accelerator programs in Latin America (they launched in 2011). At that time, the only experience I had with startup culture was while living in Santiago de Chile. I remember walking into Startup Chile's headquarters in a converted colonial building and meeting a diverse group of people sitting with their laptops under a skylight dome. . It communicated openness and creativity. People roamed around sharing ideas and getting inspired from each other. It felt like stepping through the wardrobe into Narnia.

When I moved to Argentina, I searched for a similar work environment. A friend of mine (who I'd later recognize as one of the best community builders I've ever met) introduced me to Marta Cruz, one of the co-founders of NXTP Labs, and she hired me. During my time at NXTP Labs, I hosted more than fifty events, each welcoming from fifty to three hundred guests. I managed the visitors' agendas and prepared and facilitated introductions. At times, I even hosted them. Most visitors came from Silicon Valley. Some were investors, others were researching the Buenos Aires startup ecosystem. When preparing agendas or considering who to connect with whom, I was guided by Ariel Arrieta. Besides being the founder of NXTP Labs, kickstarting the accelerator and bringing the other co-founders on board, he was also one of the earliest startup founders in Argentina, having launched his first company in the 1990s. I was unaware at the time, but through his mentorship, I was going through a practical Ecosystem Building MBA. I eventually left the accelerator to join an education tech startup, but I value my time at NXTP Labs greatly and credit Ariel and the team there for inspiring me to become an entrepreneur.

Argentina is reported by *Inc.* to be one of the toughest business climates in the world, with one of the highest corruption rates. Yet it is home to one of the first Latin American startups to trade in NASDAQ—MercadoLibre raised a US$289 million IPO in 2007. And it is not alone. In a 2016 article, the *Financial Times* described Argentina as home to the majority of Latin America's tech unicorns. The article mentions companies like Globant, OLX, and Despegar.com. I had the luck to learn directly from the founders of some of these tech companies while hosting them at Startup Grind Buenos Aires fireside chats. The Argentinean batch of founders from the 1990s would go on to become the main investors in their startup ecosystem. They would inspire, mentor, and support future founders (who were often former employees at their companies), creating what Endeavor calls a "multiplier effect." One of Latin America's largest venture capital firms to this day, Kaszek Ventures, was founded by two early employees from MercadoLibre. There is a tight correlation between past and future unicorns in Argentina.

The economic value of an abundance mindset has been studied widely, most notably the case of Silicon Valley. Why did the region become the epicenter of fast technological development in the 20th and 21st centuries? AnnaLee Saxenian is known for her work on technology clusters and social networks in Silicon Valley. In *Regional Advantage: Culture and Competition in Silicon Valley and Route 128*, she explains that the success of Silicon Valley is related to a culture of openness and sharing.

Research conducted by Startup Genome validates that economic growth is accelerated by local connectedness. That is, the amount of peer-to-peer support offered between founders. Local connectedness also includes support from experts and investors, who often have no shares nor specific interests in the company they are helping.

We will dive deeper into this topic, but for now, let's take an overview of why an abundance mindset matters.

Creating Abundance in Scarce Contexts

Scarcity drives aggressiveness, separation, and distrust.

Regardless of where you grew up, you might have experienced an environment that felt threatening. You may have felt like you had to keep both eyes open to care for yourself. Unfortunately, I find this to be especially true in emerging countries.

Having lived in Brazil, Argentina, and Malaysia for most of my life, I have seen this first-hand. There is institutionalized distrust in these places. This is what happens when a country's most relevant institutions fail. It's what happens when the institutions meant to protect you instead threaten you. When public representatives do such disservice to society, it creates a general belief in trickery and corruption. It perpetuates individualism and the idea that "if I don't care for myself, no one else will." That, allied with the need to fit in and be part of a group, leads to widespread nepotism, from company boards to politics.

It is not easy to change this mindset. I personally find it easier to start from a small group of people and grow from there, creating safe spaces, hosting recurring encounters, and building familiarity to enhance trust over time.

Fostering authentic connections (friendships, not contacts) is a key way to show and reinforce that, within this space, I care for others as they care for me. To engineer an abundant space, you must start by giving first, regardless of the perceived risks. Make people feel they can give first, knowing that everyone's success would be satisfactory for them.

If you come from a scarcity-mindset (fearful, jealous, or selfish), practice breathing deeply and looking at the big picture. When we're too focused on the trees, we lose perspective of the forest all around us. Look beyond whatever is holding you back. Go outside and distance yourself from whatever you are attached to or fighting for. Have a wider perspective of what it means. In doing so, you might find the fight is worth it, or not. We often attach ourselves to things, positions, titles, and even people that, in reality, do not belong to us.

Abundance emerges from feeling grateful for what you have while knowing it to be impermanent. It is about creating confidence that what you truly need to feel completely happy is within yourself.

Side note: if someone is trying to "steal" anything or acting unethically within your community, there are times when you must take action to kick them out. Unfortunately, at times burning bridges with scarcity minded behavior is fundamental to keeping an abundant space. We will talk about these practical and actionable steps in Part II.

Abundance is a state of mind that emerges from feeling safe enough to be your truest self, from feeling at peace to be part of something. When you feel at home, you trust good things are about to happen. Coding an abundance mindset into communities within a scarcity context means creating a safe place. It means creating a sense of home, of family, and being the first to trust. Start by giving, and let the virtuous circle continue.

Prerequisites to Manifest the AHA Core Values

A safe space is *sine qua non* for people to freely express themselves. A safe space is somewhere that people feel at home because they find in it something that feels familiar. We will dive deeper into it in the next chapter.

You can always find generous people in a scarce context. Generosity is a beautiful act that can inspire further generosity in others, who will repeat the act towards someone else in a continuous pay-it-forward fashion.

Yet, under average circumstances, abundance thrives best if it goes in all directions. Creating safe spaces is the best way to get started, in every case. When people feel safe, they feel like they can trust whoever is within that space and, consequently, they are more willing to contribute. To give first means to belong.

Actions speak louder than words. Leading by example is fundamental to implementing any value you expect your community to follow. It can lead to changing behavior through role-modeling as long as it is repeated relentlessly amongst the same group of people.

There is no chronological order between these core values. You can embed them into your community from every corner. Start anywhere and everywhere:

1. By demonstrating authenticity. It builds up trust and makes people feel that they can give first.

2. By acting humble. It shows that there is no need for power struggles or competition, and that standing out isn't what matters.

3. By practicing abundance. It inspires others to give, enhancing trust and making people feel that they can relax, open up, and share.

That's how you create a virtuous circle: from one to many.

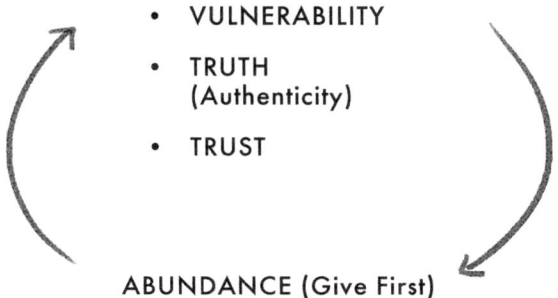

CHAPTER 6

Building Trust: Creating Safe (Vulnerable) Spaces

"Courage starts with showing up and letting ourselves be seen."

—*DARING GREATLY*, BRENÉ BROWN

Making Space for Vulnerability

Vulnerability is the preamble of great decisions as a team. When people feel comfortable to be authentic, they are more likely to speak up. When everyone feels free to speak, we make stronger decisions because there is buy-in: everyone is involved. Even though consensus might not be reached, everyone is committed. They feel responsible for the outcome. There's ownership. And when all the above is present, a team is likely to achieve whatever goal they aim to achieve.

Great decisions lead to great results. Results are the critical evidence of something greater beneath the surface: an empowered, committed, and aligned team.

Originating from vulnerability is a virtuous cycle that culminates in a distributed sense of ownership. This is well explained by the author Patrick LencionI in his book *The Five Dysfunctions of a Team*, which introduced the world to a simple and complete framework for team performance.

While Lencioni's framework applies to teams, we can lend it to communities. You can build a team as a community.

Community leadership means building trust and creating a strong sense of ownership that pushes people to act, even when nobody told them to. We will talk about the essence of leadership, which is about empowering people through stories and providing clarity. Leadership is about creating a sense of ownership around a shared vision and trusting people. The opposite of community leadership is micro-management.

Building a team as a community has a lot to do with organizational culture, but it is more than that. In another excellent book, *The Four Obsessions of an Extraordinary Executive*, LencionI presents a framework to develop culture as an asset. It starts from a strong leadership team that creates clarity, reinforces it through processes and actions, and over-communicates it on a daily basis. A company culture is not about a pretty manifesto hand-painted on the walls. It is about empowering everyone to feel like they own it. Make your Golden Circle (the why, how, and what) clear at every level and be cohesive in your actions.

A community-driven leadership style does not mean a lack of hierarchy. Nor does it mean a democratic decision-making system. Especially in companies, a leadership vision from a strategic level is fundamental.

I learned this the hard way when leading a nonprofit. I was managing around two thousand volunteers distributed in eighteen chapters across three countries: Argentina, Chile, and Uruguay. No one got paid to do their job, and we needed their job done with hard numbers to meet, from sales to fundraising, not to mention recruitment. Otherwise, the organization would die within a year.

We were planning to host a regional event in Chile. It had high fixed costs and was in a context where people had limited incomes (we had to subsidize part of the ticket costs for all the 350 youth leaders who were coming from more than twenty-five countries). Long story short: I got those two thousand people to work together. Without getting paid. They had only met each other in person two or three times a year, at conferences we had organized ourselves.

I managed to do this because our leadership was one hundred percent community-driven. We took the time to create clarity through stories that communicated our vision. We built strong leadership teams and dedicated a lot of time to developing people through coaching, mentorship, and follow-ups. We emphasized our vision, values, and goals through action. Finally, we kept a cadence of communication, never losing touch. We over-communicated everything.

Community-driven teams are those where every team member has a strong focus on the shared vision. Everyone feels ownership towards common goals. A community leader must create safe spaces to develop a team that feels empowered and genuinely cares about results.

In this chapter, I will share three stories to illustrate the path to building and keeping safe spaces.

First, we will explore why vulnerability is key to authentic connections. Then, we will learn from communities that were able to create safe spaces. Lastly, we will talk about cultural change, as many might face challenges in trying to create a community environment in a company where an authoritarian (or control freak) culture prevails.

In my journey through thirteen years of working with startups and community building, I learned that creating safe spaces is not an option, but a key step in developing leadership and building a team that works on its own.

Leading By Example

> *"Make your mess your message."*
>
> —*EVERYBODY'S GOT SOMETHING*, ROBIN ROBERTS

What do you fear that keeps you from being vulnerable?

At first, it may be hard to picture ourselves being vulnerable in a large crowd. Crowds are not community and, as such, can be scary. To build a community, we often need to dare to be the first to share our most vulnerable selves with the crowd.

Robin Roberts, a popular anchor of ABC's *Good Morning America*, is a great example of sharing vulnerability. When Hurricane Katrina hit Louisiana (where she comes from and where her family still lived), she was sent to cover its impact. Before landing, she was unable to communicate with her family. She didn't know if they were alive until she arrived at her mother's house and found them safe outside the damaged house. Soon after, she had to present on camera to communicate the impact of Katrina on national television. She showed up buttoned-up, standing strong to report the happenings. But then Charlie Gibson, her colleague hosting the show from NYC, asked her (on live TV) about her family. "Did you find them? Are they OK?" he asked. And she can't help it. She breaks into tears, breathes deep and shares that "yes, they're OK," adding that "so many people (are) affected by this storm who can't get to their loved ones. I was fortunate enough to be able to get down here and see them firsthand."

Charlie Gibson thanked her and the segment ended. Off-camera now, Robin realizes what just happened. That was it. She would be fired. She had cried on live television. Maybe if she was lucky, she could get a job back in Louisiana. Well, the exact opposite happened. She had been authentic. People could relate to that, especially in a moment when so many people were truly suffering from similar pain. She was not just another journalist, but someone who they identified with. They wanted to see more of her. In her own words, she learned that "the intent of making your mess your message is that of being of service to others, through what you've gone through." Later in her career, she applied this same perspective in publicly sharing her experience with breast cancer. She said, "I was trying to help you, and I was helped in return."

As community leaders, we need to be the first to show up. We have to speak our truth, dare to demonstrate our feelings and, in doing so, open space for others to truly connect with us.

Creating Safe Spaces: Bringing Up Lionesses

If women's sexuality is still taboo around the world, imagine starting a pole dancing community in a country where sexuality is restricted in general. In Malaysia, this community thrived bravely.

The experience I had in joining them taught me a lot about creating safe spaces where people can be vulnerable.

It was 2016 and I was in Kuala Lumpur. I climbed up the narrow stairs of a typical Malaysian shophouse. Downstairs, there was an Indian restaurant, a neighboring Malay restaurant, and a bank at the corner. On the first flight, in front of a hair salon, I rang the doorbell. The door buzzed open without a word. The next flight of stairs had pictures of beautiful women in corselets and elegant heels in sensual, classy poses displayed on the walls, boudoir-like. It was like walking into a secret, speakeasy, an alternative reality in the middle of conservative Kuala Lumpur, where some women choose to (or have to) wear a scarf.

I remember my first class. Standing in front of the mirror, looking at a pot-bellied girl in grandma underwear. That was me. When the dance started, I focused on the teacher swinging her hips side to side, up and down. Even in the warm-up, she looked hot. Each time I looked at myself in the mirror, I felt like covering up and admitting I was better off elsewhere. But my curiosity overcame my shame, and I stayed in my first pole dancing class. Around me, there were women of all shapes and sizes. Some were perfectly synced to the rhythm, some were flexible, while others were offbeat or struggled to stretch a leg. Over time, I learned to look at myself and grow to love my own body. And I learned to see the beauty of every woman's body. From being a sedentary nerd, I found myself taking a wide range of classes. From floorwork to striptease and lap dancing. Learning from women who were business owners, financial advisors, mothers, sex workers, showgirls... It didn't matter. The more confident a woman felt, the more she loved herself, and the more beautiful she looked.

To this day, pole dancing is one of my favorite activities. Traveling around the world, I would go to pole dance studios even if just for one day, from Manila to Mexico City. Suddenly, I'd be hanging upside down in my underwear around a group of women I had never seen before, one of them holding my back to save me from falling.

Pole dancing is more than just a dance. It is a self-love community, where people—not only women—learn to let themselves be seen and to appreciate their bodies, even if they might seem inadequate to the media. Together, we explore a variety of poses and shapes that show us our bodies are beautiful.

Exploring diversity within the pole dancing community was especially true in San Francisco. Shortly after I landed in the Bay Area, I enrolled at the San Francisco Pole and Dance School. Amy Bond, its founder, went from a struggling actress to having a movie-character occupation: her list of jobs includes au pair, bar dancer, English teacher, waitress, sex worker, elementary school chess teacher, textbook binder, barback, personal trainer, Zumba instructor, volunteer, startups and, more recently, pole dance studio owner and pro bono attorney.

Amy reconnected with a powerful part of herself after walking into a dark room filled with other women at her first pole dancing class. There, she re-embraced her sexuality after years of suppressing it. After working in the sex and porn industry while struggling as an actress, she was excommunicated from her original support group (her church) and dumped by her boyfriend. She felt damaged for years, until she walked into that dark room filled with women. In her words, it was the first time she explored a "sexuality that was defined by other women, for other women." It was about her sexuality for herself, not for others.

Once, I was in class with Amy. We sat on the floor, making small talk as customary at the beginning of every class. Amy hosted the circle, inviting each of us to share our name, something we wanted for today's class, and our favorite ice cream flavor. I had my back against the door, when, suddenly, Amy stood up and raged. "Nicholas, get out of here. I've seen what you've done and this is not accepted in here," she shouted. Her words were as intimidating as her posture. Standing on nine-inch heels and with an inflated chest, she looked three feet taller. "Walk out of this building right now or I'll call the cops," she thundered. The guy left.

Five of us were sitting on the floor in lingerie and seven- to nine-inch heels. I can't describe many situations where you are more vulnerable than when pole dancing.

Twice, I saw Amy rising like a lioness to protect her community. She would name wrongdoers and exclude those who had corrupted the sense of safety she had created. "We are a safe space. Literally, that is our value proposition," she told me in an interview.

A lawyer with a street-smart attitude, Amy didn't hesitate in taking action the right way. She did not allow anyone to put her community at risk, especially the safety boundaries built to make her students feel at home.

It's important not to get distracted with asking "how did she let it happen?" Bad things can happen. Wrongdoers will join great communities. The important part is how you manage crises. Nicholas was one of very few cases of some kind of harassment around her school. While Amy created a safe space, she couldn't avoid such threats creeping into her studio, but she dealt with it fiercely and assertively. In an article titled "A Wolf in Booty Shorts," she shares a story of how she dealt with a student who harassed other peers and instructors. Once it came to her awareness, she acted upon it immediately.

At the pole dancing school, the safety borders were invisible—they were held by Amy, the instructors, and every community member. Amy set the boundaries, making it easy for people to speak up, and when it felt needed, she rose like a lioness protecting her pride.

Cultural Shift: Cleaning Up the Dirt

This story illustrates how we can make practical use of a safe space to host difficult conversations, particularly to manage cultural change. It helps ground us by drawing a positive picture of how a community should work, to address complexity from this place.

It was 2011, in Mendoza, Argentina. I remember sitting at a round table in a conference room, jotting down ideas on paper. How was I going to introduce the topic and manage the discussions? I was still deciding. My hands were sweating, my heart pounding. I tried to organize my thoughts, pen on paper.

In the background, a half-circle of country flags made me think of the world. It inspired me to look at the bigger picture. I thought of world leaders trying to decide for the common good, against their own economic and political interests. I pictured the world in comparison to that room, ready to fit nineteen youth leaders from Argentina, Chile, and Uruguay in a circle of chairs. The room felt small. That thought gave me the strength to think that the encounter was not going to kill me, but teach me a bigger lesson. Besides, I had no better option.

I felt exhausted, but this thought felt like an act of faith. I had trust in what I had to do. That was the right thing.

The night before, I had slept for only three hours. I spent hours on the phone with a frustrated, screaming funding partner (aka an investor). She was the manager for a large corporate fund that had been a major donor for a social impact project, meant to supply international talent to local NGOs across Argentina, Chile, and Uruguay.

Even though I had no direct role in the project, which had been poorly delivered the year before, I had been leading all organizations for three months. Therefore, I was formally responsible for it.

Our organization received funding from this woman's fund to run the program. I was told by my former colleagues to avoid her. She had been labeled the crazy woman. In an angry monologue she talked about mismanaged funds and made borderline accusations of unethical practices. These allegations wounded me for several reasons. First, I was not aware of most of the things she accused us of. Second, I felt stupid for not being aware, and now, I was responsible for the mess. Last, but not least, we were a social impact organization. We had values and standards for performance. How could we let this happen?

The funds had been distributed across some of our eighteen local chapters across Argentina, Chile, and Uruguay. These chapters were led by young directors who ran their local teams while studying. The six-month project had been managed by even less-experienced people. I could not blame them for mismanagement, but I had to take action to correct it and make sure these mistakes would not be repeated in the future.

When I was elected as president of the NGO, this project had been finalized. Little could be done now. At the very least, I had to deliver an impact report with the little information I had available because the one delivered had not pleased our business partner.

She kept screaming. As I listened, I didn't try to argue, but understand. I asked her to clarify what she meant. The original project team had left without specifying her complaints. They painted her as a feisty, bossy woman. When her continued dissatisfaction drove her to me, I had to go beyond those labels and assess the validity of her points. I listened. At first I felt personally attacked by her, but continued listening. Then she stopped screaming.

She said, "I see your good intentions and I think you are capable of doing this. It seems like you want to make things right, but right now the organization you're leading is like a very dirty sponge. You have to squeeze the dirt out. It's going to hurt. A lot. But if you don't, you won't achieve anything good."

Indeed, the previous months had seemed impossible. I was unable to get anything done. I was extinguishing fires every day. I had almost collapsed. It couldn't go on this way. My executive team had endured attacks from some local chapter directors who demanded certain financial advantages and benefits, threatening our positions if we didn't do what they wanted. It was borderline extortion. The organization was infested by dirty politics, side talking, fragmentation, and power struggles. These were just symptoms of a deeper wound that needed cleaning before it could heal.

The thought of dealing with it felt painful. I felt responsible for the organization as if I owned it. I could feel its weight, its dirt, and almost my hands hurting when squeezing it clean.

The next morning, I told my regional team that we needed to change the agenda. I needed three hours with the eighteen local chapter executive directors. They agreed. One of them offered to be in the room with me, but something told me I had to face them on my own. My team helped to reorganize the agenda and logistics around it.

After lunch, I found myself sitting at that round table in the conference room where I started this story. Jotting down ideas on paper. I had a flipchart nearby.

I ripped out a sheet of paper and placed it on the floor at the center of the circle of chairs. I mentally composed my speech, which had to appear spontaneous and honest. I drafted the flow of the conversation in bullet points. I closed my eyes to set a clear intention of where I wanted to go.

I did not know how the conversation would go, but I was positive about where I wanted us to be.

Finally, I drew a triangle on the paper on the floor.

Soon, the executive directors started to walk in. I sat in one of the chairs, facing the flipchart. The chairs filled up. I started by reminding the room of our purpose as a nonprofit, which was of achieving peace and fulfillment of humankind's potential. We talked about what that meant in practice. It brought us to a common ground, beyond the obvious.

Next, I asked them, "how are we doing, towards our mission?"

Silence. Someone asked for a more detailed explanation.

I brought up how, in our latest meetings, we had replaced conversations about social impact with bitter arguments and power struggles. We'd argue about the commas in our regional compendium (essentially the constitution for our organization). And I made myself vulnerable. I mentioned, for the first time, that I'd been feeling inadequate as their president, but was committed to staying if they trusted me to work it out.

Some people brought up conflicts they had between each other. They cleared up gossip that was running around. Someone was accused of playing politics, but had a chance to speak about it. Another felt that we didn't care about their local chapter. Yet another felt their team was burning out and couldn't deal with it.

We started to get vulnerable.

At this point, I walked to the center of the circle and started Lencioni's triangle. I explained it from the dysfunctional point of view:

"When there is no vulnerability, there is a false sense of harmony. That leads to conflict avoidance. The outcome? Dissatisfaction becomes side talking and politics. Exactly what we're doing now."

They were silent. Some nodded.

I continued, "What happens then is we don't make authentic decisions. We hold back when we get a chance to share. So, when we finally make a decision, some don't feel part of it. When we go back home to our chapters, we tell them our version. Those who did not buy in (or speak up) will refrain from working towards the goals we set. They won't take action or push their teams to do so. As a whole, we can't deliver."

At this point, everyone was staring in silence. I ended with, "When we finally get back to the conference, our morale is low. We created a low standard across the board. We avoid pushing others harder because we are afraid of being criticized as well. We separate ourselves from the vision and the organization to feel better. We point fingers, blame others, justify our actions, and give excuses rather than owning our responsibilities."

I stopped and asked, "Do you recognize this?"

They could see our reality translated into the framework. It was not about them and their shame anymore, but something bigger. It was about everyone and they were part of it. They started talking, sharing their perspectives. I wrapped up to give them a quick overview of the virtuous cycle of the model, presenting what happens when we start from vulnerability.

"If we feel safe to be vulnerable, we communicate authentically," I said. "We make genuine decisions. All cards on the table. We make honest commitments. We buy in and can sell it, spreading the word to our local chapters. Next time we come back together, it is more likely that we will have acted on it. We are not ashamed, but ready to talk about what we've done, the results we had, and how it could have been better."

From there, we shared an idea of how things could be better. We stood on common ground. On one side, we agreed things were bad. We needed to change. We also had a wider, positive perspective of how we could be if we decided to speak up and make genuine decisions.

I proposed that we get vulnerable to clear the dirt, for once and for all. Recalling Robin Roberts's advice, I made my mess my message.

I shared how inadequate I felt, how the whole situation affected my performance and that of the regional executive team as a consequence. I revealed how the situation with the mismanaged project deeply hurt me. I also said that I'd love to get through this, to learn with them to become a better leader, and to continue walking together.

Next thing I know, everyone was sharing. My job was to listen, hold space, and facilitate the conversations to guarantee everyone shared a bit.

At the end of the session, we admitted it was hard to fix the existing relationship between us. They had only three more months left on the executive teams for their local chapters, but we committed to clear the dirt for their successors, creating a safe space for their replacements to be more vulnerable, honest, responsible, and collaborative from the get-go. As our last project together, we got to create a safe space for the next generation to be better leaders. No politics. No side talking. No fragmentation. We committed to change the culture by exposing our differences. We squeezed the dirty sponge together. What happened next?

From there, side talks stopped. The fight for power did too. We started discussing projects, ideas, acknowledging areas where we needed to improve. We decided that anything worth saying was worth sharing with everyone. Our next conference (and last conference together), we celebrated the end of the year with a great party. Two leaders from that group then joined my regional team, which helped integrate all of us.

Their successors were the most collaborative team of chapter leaders I have had the privilege to witness. Conversations were around joint projects that could boost regional growth. They talked to each other with brutal honesty, holding the common good in mind. One year later, the regional executive team that came to lead the region after mine achieved nearly 150 percent growth in sales and recruitment.

I could share more about it, but in essence, what we achieved was a cultural shift. We dared to speak authentically, helped by a framework written on a sheet of paper on the floor.

And that was just the beginning.

Connecting the Dots: Vulnerability as the Root to Great Results

Let's look at the main lessons from the three stories above.

- Make your mess your message. Be the first one to take the courageous step to be seen as your most authentic self.

- Create a safe space where everyone can be vulnerable, regardless of the context around it. Then, maintain this space by always listening and acting fast when anything seems to threaten that sense of safety.

- Dare to host difficult conversations. You must be the one to start, even if it seems risky. Keeping the community safe and sane is your responsibility.

Vulnerability is the root of authentic communication and effective decision-making. This path leads to commitment, ownership, responsibility, and alignment towards common goals.

Without creating a safe space where you and your community feel comfortable to show up and be seen, you will likely have a false sense of harmony. People may continue to work hard, have meetings, and pretend that everything is ok, but from there, commitments slip through the cracks and your whole vision falls down a steep slope.

We need courage and trust to engage in difficult conversations. We need trust to endure through conflict with others. That is made possible by creating a safe space, and a leader speaking vulnerably could be the start of that space.

As a leader, you must not create, but also maintain a safe space. Hopefully, you will not need to go through the pain of squeezing the dirty sponge, but if it is ever necessary, you must be the one taking action first.

In Part II, we will dive deeper into the practice of building trust and creating safe spaces with frameworks that will guide you through the process.

CHAPTER 7

Sharing (Anything): Cultivating an Abundance Mindset

"My goal is to life as happy an existence on this planet as I can and, by giving before I get, I maximize my chance of this"

—"GIVE BEFORE YOU GET," BRAD FELD

Why an Abundance Mindset?

The essence of communities is in sharing: food, shelter, and resources, as well as values, knowledge, and ideas. Sharing translates to optimization. The same resource (concrete or abstract) has its value multiplied when it is useful to a diverse group of people.

Sharing is one of the main reasons why building communities is not only good for our health but also good for economic reasons. An abundance mindset has been fundamental to the development of some of the most successful startup ecosystems in the world, including Silicon Valley.

We'll talk about the economic impact of a culture of abundance by looking at some of the fastest-growing startup ecosystems worldwide. Research and evidence-based insights from AnnaLee Saxenian to Startup Genome will help us illustrate this idea.

We will also understand what an abundance mindset means from an individual's perspective. As a community builder, it is crucial to practice abundance to create a context for sharing. It is also crucial to create ownership, encouraging people to speak of your brand as if it was their own. The consequence of doing so is organic growth.

Some of the largest startup communities on the global level have abundance-related values in their list. "Give > Take" for Startup Grind. "Give First" for Techstars.

These communities have achieved grassroots growth on a global level, spreading chapters all over the world. They empower their leaders with the idea of abundance, by defining it with a simple action ("give"). But there's more to it. They select people who already have a practical notion of abundance. I know this from my personal experience of interviewing potential chapter leaders. Good candidates were those who were already giving and adding value to their communities. They reinforced their purported values through actions, by enabling their peers. They created tools, platforms, and "to-dos" to help their community leaders give and add value first. For a community to grow through its people, it is fundamental to make sure they share these core values.

In this chapter, we will examine how abundance is the key to exponential growth and how it helps to spread a sense of ownership. Communities only grow fast by trusting their members to spread the word, and this only happens when founders are confident to give their members the power and tools to do so.

Finally, we will talk about what it takes to create an abundance mentality in scarce environments, because it is impossible to ask people to share their ideas or resources if they don't feel safe to do so. To build abundance, trust is preeminent.

Creating safe spaces where people can be vulnerable allows authenticity. Safe spaces also help people to act from abundance. When they feel supported, they are more willing to help each other.

The Rising Tide Lifts All Boats

When I landed in Malaysia, I was looking forward to integrating myself in its startup scene. I had learned the best way to do this back in Buenos Aires, where I hosted Startup Grind and worked at one of the top accelerators in Latin America. I knew that to be a meaningful part of Malaysia's startup scene, I had to add value first.

> **About Startup Grind**
>
> Startup Grind is a global startup community focused on strengthening local communities. Founded in 2010 in Silicon Valley, it hosts monthly gatherings that bring together local entrepreneurs, talent, and investors, and facilitates connections between them. Each meetup serves both as a mass-mentoring session where seasoned founders are interviewed, and as a means to attract the entire community to one place every month, especially serving as a lighthouse to newcomers. When I joined Startup Grind by starting the Buenos Aires chapter, in 2012, there were around twenty chapters worldwide. Today, there are over six hundred.

I decided to start a Startup Grind chapter in my new city of Kuala Lumpur. Before that, I explored a little to see what was happening in the scene, mapping most of its existing communities (events, accelerators, coworking spaces, and alike) and inviting some local leaders for coffee. Most of these conversations were warm welcomes and I made some good friends. Later, we built ourselves a small community: co-hosting events, going for beers, sharing best practices and connections.

But a few people advised me not to start another meetup. A lot was going on already, they said. There were not enough people attending. Some didn't even want to meet a "competitor." I even got my first venue request denied because the space was hosting another meetup that competed with Startup Grind.

Before I go on, I want to remind you that in community building, and especially in ecosystem development, abundance rules all. There might be competing meetups and companies, but if space gets small, the goal is not to kill others who threaten you, but to widen the space. Reach more people. Break bubbles. Make yourself better.

Regardless of the negative feedback, I wanted to run Startup Grind as a way to give first. No one was interviewing Malaysia's seasoned founders and that was an evident gap. It was a missed opportunity to share knowledge. I decided to keep going despite a few warnings that there were too many events in town.

I hosted the first Startup Grind Kuala Lumpur in March 2014. Sixty people attended. At the next event, we had seventy-five. Then the third attracted 250 guests, which was a lot for a meetup—too much even. Holding on to the mentality of adding value beyond what already existed, we made it different to other events. For catering, we partnered with local food entrepreneurs to spotlight their brands. We partnered with up-and-coming spaces that needed visibility as event venues. We promoted other events happening in town.

Within three months, Startup Grind Kuala Lumpur became a placemaking machine. Every venue wanted to host us (for free). Others offered food and freebies. I started hosting more events: private dinners between foreign investors and local founders, coworking days, cozy brunch sessions for other community builders. I also ran a weekly newsletter promoting all the local events.

In six months, I was hired by the Malaysian government as a community ambassador consultant to help them build a more cohesive ecosystem, connecting their programs to the grassroots. A year later, I started my first business (acquired in 2016): an online marketplace for flexible work and event spaces. It was built on the large portfolio of spaces and people I got to know through hosting events. Most of my clients were large companies (including Heineken, KPMG, and even Google) that were willing to get their employees out of the office for a bit.

Eventually, I started other communities: one for B2B founders and another for women in science, technology, and business. But more than that, I made a lot of friends.

What did I learn from this? I learned that through starting something from the genuine willingness of adding value and helping others (who thought of themselves as competitors), I was able to build a larger community for everyone. I learned that the rising tide lifts all boats.

Abundance Mindset in Scarcity Contexts

At one of the interviews I hosted, a seasoned entrepreneur said that if we had one thing to copy from Silicon Valley to make any ecosystem successful, it was the mindset of abundance. He explained how in Malaysia, people were often scarcity-driven. A context of poverty and corruption created a sense that if they did not take care of themselves, no one would. People would help themselves first, rather than help each other.

I can relate to that. Being born and raised in Brazil, having lived in Mauritius, Argentina, and Malaysia, I have witnessed a pervasive sense of distrust. In these places, the abundance mindset is often restricted to familiar contexts: friends and family. In some cases, it extends to a geographical community (people help their neighborhoods, but not beyond).

Regardless of your context, whether an emerging economy or not, if there is scarcity, an abundance mindset can only be engineered by giving first. This is most easily done when its demonstrated by a core group of people who already believe in it. We will dive deeper into how to engineer an abundance mindset in scarce contexts in Part II. For now, let's take a look at some examples of how this mindset yields positive results.

The Economic Value of Abundance-Mindset

Silicon Valley and Stockholm

In the 1970s, Silicon Valley and Boston's Route 128 shared a position as the world's leading centers of technological innovation, entrepreneurship, and economic growth. In the 1980s, both regions faced critical challenges (for different reasons). In her book Regional Advantage, AnnaLee Saxenian says, "It appeared that America's high technology industry, once seen as invulnerable, might not survive the challenge of intensified international competition."

But while specialists expected its downfall, Silicon Valley was able to reinvent itself, responding fast to competition with new technology brought up by emerging startups.

Today, Silicon Valley maintains its crown as the most relevant startup ecosystem in the world, largely surpassing the runner-ups: London and New York City. According to Startup Genome's *Global Startup Ecosystem Report 2020*, Silicon Valley's startup ecosystem boasts an value of US$677 billion, while London and New York City are far behind at US$92 billion and US$147 billion respectively.

How was Silicon Valley able to keep its competitive edge, while Route 128 took longer to regain relevance? AnnaLee Saxenian explains:

> Silicon Valley has a regional network-based industrial system that promotes collective learning and flexible adjustment among specialist producers of a complex of related technologies. The region's dense social networks and open labor markets encourage experimentation and entrepreneurship. Companies compete intensely while at the same time learning from one another about changing markets and technologies through informal communication and collaborative practices; and loosely linked team structures encourage horizontal communication among firm divisions and with outside suppliers and customers.

Saxenian goes on to quote Tom Wolfe, who says in his article "The Tinkerings of Robert Noyce: How the sun rose on the Silicon Valley" that "it wasn't enough to start up a company; you had to start a community, a community in which there were no social distinctions, and it was first come, first served in the parking lot, and everyone was supposed to internalize the common goals."

Wolfe describes the influence of the Fairchild Semiconductor Corporation in fostering a community-driven management style (which shocked executives from the East Coast). Several companies emerging from Fairchild shared similar core values. According to Saxenian, "similar shared professional experiences continued to reinforce the sense of community in the region even after individuals had moved on to different, often competing, firms." She adds that "to this day, a poster of the Fairchild family tree, showing the corporate genealogy of the scores of Fairchild spin-offs, hangs on the walls of many Silicon Valley firms." A similar impact would be observed in the future with the "PayPal Mafia." PayPal mushroomed into Tesla, LinkedIn, SpaceX, Square, YouTube, Yelp, and others. The same was seen in other ecosystems. A 2012 study by Endeavor Argentina described how the Argentinian startup ecosystem flourished from its early companies through what it termed "the multiplier effect."

Why does it matter? These companies embedded the mindset of openness and collaboration that would later influence the success of the ecosystems where they emerged.

The economic impact of collaboration is revealed in Startup Genome research, which identified that more locally and globally connected startup ecosystems demonstrate better performance, at a faster pace. Local connectedness is defined as the level of support being provided from founder to founder, as well as by experts and investors. Global connectedness is defined as the number of quality connections reported by local founders in top startup ecosystems worldwide when quality is defined by the possibility to text, email, or call a peer and receive not only a response but a conversation or an introduction or a reference.

For instance, strong relationships with other founders are strongly associated with higher startup performance, taking into account two measures: employment and sales. Startups with low-connected founders have, on average, lower employment than startups that are better connected. A higher number of local relationships is correlated with higher sales.

Global connections accelerate founders' experience. Tapping into a global fabric of ideas, talent, capital, and know-how leads to faster revenue growth and accelerates the growth of the ecosystem. More globally connected startups become scale-ups at a faster pace by growing their global market reach from the get-go.

In a nutshell, Silicon Valley has grown as the epicenter of startup ecosystems worldwide thanks to an abundance mindset, translated into a culture of openness and collaboration. Even though its culture has changed over time, its influence has spread throughout the world, inspiring places like Stockholm (which has the highest number of unicorns per capita in the world after Silicon Valley, according to a 2015 Wharton University study).

With this success linked to an abundance mindset, it should not come as a surprise that some of the largest startup communities in the world, such as Techstars and Startup Grind, highlight "Give First" and "Give > Take" among their core values.

The Abundance Mindset in Practice

Practicing Gratitude and Welcoming Impermanence

What does it take for you to give first? A safe space. It takes a sense of belonging. It takes people feeling glad to be part of something (humility). It takes people feeling that what is good for the whole is good for themselves as well. Feeling welcome, accepted, seen, and cared for as you are (authenticity) makes it easier for anyone to share anything. All of these factors are prerequisites for people to feel abundant.

But as a community builder, you can't expect those prerequisites to be present. When starting a community, you must be the one to set the tone. Start by giving first.

I believe that most people are intrinsically abundance-minded and it is just a matter of activating it. But we're often born into circumstances where we don't get to practice it. For example, if we're born and raised in a context where we don't feel safe around others, how do we activate the capacity to think and act abundantly?

It works for me to stand on the shoulders of giants; to be around abundance-minded people. This doesn't necessarily mean hanging out with them in the same room—it could even be reading about them, listening to interviews, or connecting with their way of thinking through other means. The more you incorporate the mindset of abundance, the harder it gets to settle for scarcity.

Abundance is where we came from. At the very beginning, our species survived thanks to belonging to communities where sharing came as an advantage. Unfortunately, most of our civilization grew upon another concept, where not everyone felt part of the same playing field. Still, at our core, we are wired to belong. It feels good to trust others. It feels good to feel at home with others and receive their gratitude when we give them something.

While working at Startup Genome, I had the opportunity to visit and research various startup ecosystems renowned for outstanding performance. I tried to decode the mindset and culture behind them.

Stockholm is a favorite. Not due to the city's amazing unicorn per capita rate, but because of the values they share. In several interviews, I found cohesion when asking local founders, VCs, and ecosystem builders about what makes that rate happen. I could sum it up in what they call the "IKEA mindset," which is largely spread and known to influence most Swedish startups, from Skype to Spotify. The basic idea is that, "if I can create a great product, at an affordable price, for millions of people around the world, why wouldn't I?"

Many people explain the success of Stockholm by looking at its size and pointing out the obvious: due to a small market, founders there had no option but to reach out to a global market to grow. That's true, and even the Swedes would agree. Their ancestors had made them predetermined to explore the world—from the Vikings to Ericsson, some would say. But there are other small markets worldwide that do not perform the same. There is more to Stockholm.

It happens that IKEA's idea creates a great business model. It builds global businesses. It starts from trying to help everyone. It is based on solving a problem for as many people as possible, instead of on trying to maximize profits on every transaction. And that creates positive outcomes for everyone involved.

Abundance on a Daily Basis

The idea that I can grow by adding value to others is a great example of an abundance mindset. Here's a list of other ways abundance-minded people think and act:

- Being grateful for what you have and welcoming it while being aware of impermanence. Trusting and being open to new circumstances.

- Expecting less. Staying humble and recognizing that the idea of "this too shall pass" applies for everything, including abundant and scarce moments in life.

- Knowing that you are here to contribute and that the more you give to others, the more you get. But that you must give and contribute without expecting anything in return.

Thinking abundantly comes with practice. Sticking to it with discipline and relentlessly is fundamental as a community leader. Over time, your community will validate the benefits of this way of working together, making it easier to act abundantly and even making it hard to act differently.

CHAPTER 8

The Rise of Authenticity: Brands are Conversations

"Successful or not, a sincere approach is the only way."

—PROVERB

Why Authenticity?

Authenticity is good for business. It is fundamental to building trust. When you build a brand with a strong core, everything you say and do resembles you. It becomes easier and natural to deliver the promise.

Authenticity allows you to build relationships, not transactions. It is about making friends, not contacts. By focusing on real bonds, you enhance loyalty. It is no longer about selling at a better price or convenience but about bringing people together for a sustained reason. It is no longer about compromising to fit it, but about true connections.

In *The Gifts of Imperfection*, Brené Brown says, "Authenticity is the daily practice of letting go of who we think we're supposed to be and embracing who we are."

Authenticity is about energy efficiency. When you are authentic, you spend less time and energy wondering how to act or what to say. Acting from your core, you build up energy as you move instead of burning fuel. Further, when you act from your truth, rewarding outcomes are a natural consequence. As the proverb goes: "Successful or not, a sincere approach is the only way."

More often than not, when you act in an authentic way, you start to attract the right people. You don't need to convince people who already believe what you believe. It's a matter of finding people who share your beliefs and communicating your value.

In Chapter 4, we read that the difference between belonging and fitting in lies in authenticity. And in Chapter 5, that becoming yourself is a journey, not a destination. Let's connect the dots now.

Brands are Conversations

Authenticity is key to building trust. In a world where information flows rapidly, authenticity is not only the best way to build a brand, but also the safest way. You can no longer sustain an inconsistent argument or insincere message for too long. Everyone is looking, listening, and watching. The more successful you grow, the more people will talk about you. If you are building a community, this is an advantage, not a threat.

Hugh Mason went from BBC London to building one of the first startup accelerators in Singapore (JFDI Asia). The contrast between his two experiences lies in centralization. While at the BBC, Mason and his team created TV shows to entertain about ten million people from an authoritative place. At JFDI Asia, Mason and his co-founder did not place themselves at the center of the community. Rather, he says that they "facilitated the community to come together." His community in Singapore became a cohesion point for the entire Southeast Asia community.

Mason explains that "in the old world, you created the conversation, you owned the brand, and if people got messages about your brand wrong, you sued them. In the modern world, the world is going to talk about your brand. You can choose to enter that conversation, but you can't control it." He reinforces that "brands are conversations," a concept from *The Cluetrain Manifesto*, a visionary piece of business literature published in the 1990s that announced "the end of business as usual." In a similar vein, Jeff Bezos said that "your brand is what people say about you when you're not in the room."

You can't pretend to be someone else and expect to sail through smooth waters. First, because access to information is widespread. The majority of the world's population walk around with a computer that fits in their pockets. Second, because that makes communication more complex as you grow. When you're inauthentic, your brand is more likely to lose cohesion.

In Chapter 12, we will talk about creating an authentic brand, which means adopting frameworks that help you communicate your core. It involves creating a character and crafting stories that others can relate to. But these are not fictional stories—it is your story (or that of your company) that people who matter want to hear. Trusting people to speak about your brand is not an option. They will talk about it anyway, so make sure they're saying the right things.

Being at Home with Yourself

> *"Authenticity is a collection of choices that we have to make every day. It's about the choice to show up and be real. The choice to be honest. The choice to let our true selves be seen."*
>
> —*THE GIFTS OF IMPERFECTION*, BRENÉ BROWN

The advice to "be yourself" has become white noise or a buzzword. I get what the words mean, but it no longer communicates something practical.

Everything around us influences who we are, who we become, especially our environment growing up. We're often a consequence of the context we live in: our family and friends, work, and school, besides everything we see on social media. But there's more to us. We are wired to connect. The search to belong is often the search for our true identity, the search for the place where we are at home while being ourselves. But what if we don't even know who that is?

Unfortunately, most of us spend a lifetime searching or settling to fit in. In the 21st century, when technology provides (most of) us with access to information and travel is accessible and our means to belong anywhere, we have fewer excuses to settle in a situation that doesn't feel comfortable. Over time, you either grow tired of the fitting-in games, or you learn to recognize when you feel whole without anyone's approval. You learn that being authentic feels better. True belonging brings a sense of being safe and grounded instead of struggling to fit in to please others. It feels like coming home to yourself. Coming home to a hot shower after a tiring day, relaxing into the feeling that, here, nothing can harm you.

The moment you notice what being yourself feels like, you learn to find the way back to this feeling. The moment you find people who truly resonate with you, who not only accept but reinforce who you are, there is no way to go back to fitting in. When you are surrounded by people who truly get you, you experience what true belonging means. This is a privilege and it is your responsibility to honor it by making space for others to express themselves authentically too.

> *"Choosing authenticity means:*
> - *cultivating the courage to be imperfect, to set boundaries, and to allow ourselves to be vulnerable;*
> - *exercising the compassion that comes from knowing that we are all made of strength and struggle; and*
> - *nurturing the connection and sense of belonging that can only happen when we believe we are strong enough.*
>
> *Authenticity demands wholehearted living and loving—even when it's hard, even when we're wrestling with the shame and fear of not being good enough, and especially when the joy is so intense that we're afraid to let ourselves feel it.*
> *Mindfully practicing authenticity during our most soul-searching struggles is how we invite grace, joy, and gratitude into our lives."*
>
> —*THE GIFTS OF IMPERFECTION*, BRENÉ BROWN

Acting from Your Core

Finding your core is the beginning of authentic connections.

When your starting point is the "why," you are capable of establishing deeper connections with people who go to the core. It sustains connections towards "why we stay together." I call it communicating from your core (which refers both to seed and heart).

The power of knowing and communicating your core is that you expand your capabilities of connection. You expand the possibilities for relating to others. Yet, your why is yours, unique, like fingerprints. We all share similar patterns, but we all have our own. Moving from your core is like moving the engines of a powerhouse.

Behind every action, there is a decision defined by your values. What do you prioritize, choose, prefer, avoid, judge? Similarly, only you can influence people's actions by understanding what matters to them. Your actions define the culture you build, but actions are defined by values. Only you can build your ideal culture by having the (first) set of values that lead to it.

VALUES > DECISIONS > ACTIONS

I repeat to you the advice Polonius gave to his son in *Hamlet*: "This, above all: to thine own self be true."

Acting from your core is the beginning of authentic relationships. Your ultimate goal is to empower people to share and spread your core, like a dandelion spreading its seed on the ground and multiplying, growing wherever it finds fertile ground. We'll talk about this more in the next chapter.

When your community grows beyond you, you will know you've done a great job.

CHAPTER 9

Letting Grow: Humility

"Sitting quietly, doing nothing, spring comes, and the grass grows, by itself."

—MATSUO BASHŌ

Another Bird in the Flock

Some people define belonging as a sense that you are part of something bigger than yourself. I like that definition, and it is exactly how I understand humility.

Being humble is being aware that, while you are aware of your value, you understand that you are just another bird in the flock. Belonging is only true when feeling part of the flock feels great, comfortable, and like home. When you finally find a place where you feel safe, seen, and cared for, you realize that you don't need to fight nor force yourself to fit in. You are free to be authentic and sure to be accepted. True belonging comes with inevitable humility.

When you truly belong, the community's well-being matters as much as yours as an individual. As we've discussed in earlier chapters, when we feel safe to be vulnerable, we tend to communicate authentically, which contributes to making decisions that we feel part of, enhancing our sense of commitment towards the whole. Belonging comes with a sense of safety, which comes with embedded vulnerability, which favors authenticity, effective decision-making, and commitment towards the collective. Being able to step into vulnerability is crucial to being a community member, and even more so for a community leader. Feeling part of, not separate from, the rest is the first step.

I believe that being humble does not exclude the awareness of your value. It doesn't mean you are not worthy or unimportant. Humility comes with knowing that you are extremely valuable, special, and important to the community, just as everyone else is (to paraphrase Margaret Mead). Because every snowflake is unique, but one on its own wouldn't make snow happen.

Being humble means to care for the greater good, knowing that you are a part of it. It reminds you that you don't own the community, even though you might have created the brand that brought them together. Some people already belong together. Your job is to communicate value and create a common ground where they can connect.

The Humble Leader

> "I wouldn't coax the plant if I were you.
> Such watchful nurturing may do it harm.
> Let the soil rest from so much digging
> And wait until it's dry before you water it.
> The leaf's inclined to find its own direction;
> Give it a chance to seek the sunlight for itself.
> Much growth is stunted by too careful prodding,
> Too eager tenderness.
> The things we love we have to learn to leave alone."
>
> —"WOMAN WITH FLOWER," NAOMI LONG MADGETT

What picture comes to mind, when you think of a leader?

We've been showered with the idea of leaders as individuals standing on pedestals. We are showered with pictures of leaders looking straight ahead with stiff shoulders, crossed arms, and solid, wide open legs, like Superman. It seems to be true that power posing can boost your self-confidence. Evidence shows up to a twenty percent testosterone increase and a relevant decrease in cortisol, according to Amy Cuddy's popular TED Talk "Your Body Language May Shape Who You Are." But while it can help you through a job interview, posing won't sustain leadership. That must come from deeper within.

There are multiple ways to look like a leader. My late grandma looked like one. She rocked soft white hair and kind but sharp dark eyes. She hosted amazing dinners for her eleven children and their extended families, which amounted to more than sixty people at a regular dinner table. Along with my grandfather, she managed to raise her children to become caring and responsible adults who subsequently raised their families with love. My grandmother was an amazing host.

She wouldn't beg, nor require everyone to sit at the dinner table by 7 pm. She had no strict agenda. She had no agenda at all. She would create a cozy space, get the table ready, and let people organize themselves. It was an organic agenda. A beautifully organized mess of grandchildren and great-grandchildren finding their way around. Everyone was fed. Everyone played. Everyone's needs seemed met. And grandmother was, in essence, a great hostess.

I like to think of community builders as hosts. They make the invitation and set up the space to welcome people, who will get together and do the magic. They create the space and then let people be. They might invite someone to give a speech while keeping it casual. They might connect people, but not stand between conversations. They could be the one who facilitates the conversation between everyone around it, or they could be the quiet one, discreetly clearing the cups from the floor when the music starts, allowing everyone to dance carelessly.

Hosts are happy to see the magic happening around them. Being a good host is about allowing people to enjoy themselves and feel at home, dancing and connecting.

Community leaders are humble. They know how to be a part of something bigger, and that anything that benefits the whole community is also good for them. This doesn't mean that, as a community leader, that you can't power pose.

You can, even more so if you're somehow shy and need that confidence boost before giving a short speech or calling someone out about something delicate.

But remember that the community leader is the host. They create a space where the community happens, making no big deal of it. Yet, they are aware of their importance. Their role is to create excuses to bring people together and foster an environment where others feel safe to be vulnerable and make authentic connections.

A community leader never forgets what matters: the connections around the table.

Dandelion Blast

Growing Grassroots, Like Cultivating Dandelions

> *"Simple and fresh and fair from winter's close emerging,*
> *As if no artifice of fashion, business, politics, had ever been,*
> *Forth from its sunny nook of shelter'd grass—innocent, golden, calm as the dawn,*
> *The spring's first dandelion shows its trustful face."*
>
> —"THE FIRST DANDELION," WALT WHITMAN.

Dandelions are among the most badass plants. They grow anywhere—through the cracks on the sidewalk, on just-mowed grass. I'd say dandelions are the plant version of the honey badger (listed as the "most fearless animal in the world" by the *Guinness Book of Records*).

I use a "dandelion blast" metaphor for community building. It is based on the simple idea of how a dandelion spreads through its flying seeds and grows without needing to be planted. You get it. Everyone who's seen bright yellow spotlights spread out on the lawn knows that spring's first dandelion won't be the last. Each fluffy ball can carry hundreds of seeds. As it grows through summer, each plant has the potential to multiply into about five thousand seeds a year.

People are as organic as plants. We take time to grow, but once we start, communities can grow at an exponential rate. As community leaders, we want to reap the benefits of organic growth. For that, we must cultivate the soil for our ideas to grow. And most importantly, we must trust people to help us spread our seeds (our core) to the world.

Here are some facts about dandelions that appeal to my inner nerd and extend on this metaphor):

- Dandelions are part of the *Asteraceae* family (from the Ancient Greek *aster*, meaning "star," due to its star-like shape).

- With over 32,000 species, this family is only rivaled in number by *Orchidaceae*. Let's say, they ended up having a lot of kids.

- The *Asteraceae* bear their flowers in *capitula*, which consist of a few or many individual flowers. The *capitulum* is a special type of inflorescence in which anything from a small cluster to hundreds or sometimes thousands of flowers are grouped to form a single flower-like structure. So what I used to think was one single flower is a community of flowers, each with a different function, yet all carrying reproductive capacities.

- In short, every plant in the *Asteraceae* family has a maximized reproductive system, from its furry seed balls to its composite flowers. So what? Here's what can we learn from dandelions and all their cousins:

- Prepare your seeds with a strong core: the "why we gather" (values, belief, purpose).

- Start from a core group, even if this is very small (the people who share your core beliefs).

- Grow by empowering and building trust. Letting people fly out and spread your core.

In Part II, we will talk about concrete actions and examples based on these three steps.

To bring the metaphor back to earth, let's look at an example. Steve Munroe went from peacemaking at the UN to placemaking. He is one of the co-founders of the first coworking space in Bali, Hubud (Hub in Ubud).

Steve and I had a conversation about how BalI became a destination for digital nomads. Much like how spring's first dandelion shows its trustful face, Hubud spread thousands of members around the world, in addition to helping and inspiring new coworking spaces to emerge around the island, which used to be a popular destination for spring holidays and weddings.

How did this happen? In 2014, Hubud's co-founders idealized the space and started building a community even before it started. They put some events together and gave the mic for people to share. Talks and workshops were delivered by community members, not by the Hubud co-founders. They started by looking to the community.

Steve says that "someone told me that who you hire first at a coworking space will determine who your first ten members are. Your first ten members will dictate who your next one hundred members are. And these one hundred will determine who you are forever." According to Steve, there is some truth to this.

Hubud's co-founders created space for people to show up and be seen. They did not control who would be there. They just attracted people by the type of space and activities on offer. The first members invited others, and the community grew.

In 2020, BalI is not only about Hubud, but about different places in other locations, serving different communities of people who want to work remotely. It is a no-brainer: BalI is a go-to place for digital nomads.

Cultivating Dandelions

My experience cultivating an abundance mindset in scarce contexts relates to cultivating dandelions. When trying to change a culture or mindset, I advise starting from a small group of people who already believe in what you believe. Creating a brand from a strong core and growing from it might lead you further. Start with believers. Get them to reinforce each others' beliefs and grow stronger as a group. They will attract others who, deep inside, always wanted to believe in the same.

As Margaret Mead said, "Never doubt that a small group of thoughtful, committed citizens can change the world. Indeed, it is the only thing that ever has."

Ruben Nieuwenhuis, one of the founders of StartupAmsterdam, advises avoiding naysayers from the start. Along with his team, he and his cofounders drove initiatives that mobilized the entire Dutch capital's startup ecosystem to accelerate its growth. In 2019, Amsterdam rose four levels in the Global Startup Ecosystems Ranking.

In a nutshell, gathering a small group of people who share your core values can change the world faster than organizing a "why we need to change the world" conference to thousands of skeptics.

Be the first dandelion, then trust people will fly out and spread your core. Remember that while you might have created the brand, space, and the initial excuses to bring them together, the reason they stay connected belongs to everyone. The core belongs to the community.

PART 2

THE ART

CHAPTER 10

Defining Community Hacking

What is Community Building? What is Community Hacking?

Community hacking is:

1. Cracking the code to thriving communities by bringing to life a core a set of principles, values and methodologies.

2. Building a self-growing community from a strong core or source code, defined by the values of abundance, humility and authenticity.

3. Accelerating trust and creating a collective sense of belonging by bringing people together consistently; facilitating relationships, not transactions.

What differentiates a community from a crowd? As discussed earlier, I define community as "people sharing (anything) consistently, regardless of their location, nationality, gender, ethnicity, or sexual orientation."

Community hacking is the compound of principles and techniques described in this book to empower individuals and organizations to create self-developing communities, grounded in the core values of abundance, humility, and authenticity.

Community building and community hacking are about creating safe spaces where people can build trust through recurring interaction. Trust is created when people share a sense of safety, sparking familiarity. The more people can relate to others in a space, the more they feel safe to be vulnerable. The more we know each other, the safer we feel to speak up authentically.

In Part I, we focused on laying the foundations for community building.

In Part II, we will share practical steps to actually build or grow a community.

Three Pillars: Connectedness, Identity, and Growth

What differentiates a community from a crowd? And how does community building differ from traditional marketing? As discussed in Part I, community building stands out in various ways. In short, we can say that it is defined by the following:

- **It is relationship-driven. Conversations move in all directions.** It is not a linear monologue. It is about participation over promotion.

- **What brings people together doesn't matter as much as the connections around it.** The focus is on the people. Even if you are selling a product or service, it serves as a "point of interaction." The main value is beyond the product or service—it's from people to people (P2P).

- **The people in your community choose to be a part of it for reasons beyond cost or convenience.** They share common core beliefs and connect to others who do so too, as long as cohesive communication is maintained.

There are three elements indicating if your group is a community or just another agglomeration (a crowd, a customer base, or a Cool Kids Club):

- Connectedness
- Identity
- Growth

Connectedness

To be deemed a community, value must be added beyond anything concrete offered (whether a product or service): from people to people (P2P). Community building is about conversations. Traditional marketing is about a one-sided speech (advertising). The first builds relationships and the second, transactions. For a community to form, it is assumed there are elements that draw people together consistently, allowing them to get to know each other and stay in touch. In Chapter 14, we will learn about the three Cs of connectedness: consistency, cadence, and cohesion.

Identity

This is the element of belonging, when people feel glad to be part of something bigger. It gives them a sense of freedom and safety. People feel comfortable to express their most authentic selves while feeling held by others, like they've got their back. Value is added from people to people. Identity adds value by offering individuals a platform of self-expression through others. Identity is a core element to community building because it empowers people to speak on your behalf. By feeling part of something, we feel responsible for it.

Growth

Participation is more relevant than promotion. Organic growth is characteristic of communities, because people who relate to you and share your core feel ownership of your shared community. Ambassadorship comes naturally.

Communities don't immediately grow from one to one thousand, but instead grow progressively from one person to another. From one to two, then three, five, twenty-one, fifty-five, in a golden ratio-like progression. Their growth follows a natural order, which can help them sustain better in the long-term. Don't take this to mean that if you are building a community around a product or service, you should not invest in targeted marketing campaigns. These should be complementary to your attraction strategy (which we will discuss in Chapter 16).

Identifying the Current Stage of Your Community

To assess how much of a community you have created or are a part of, consider your organization and respond to the following statements using the scale 1 = Disagree, 2 = Not sure, 3 = Strongly agree.

The purpose of this (simple) questionnaire is self-reflection, not assessing the value of your community. From here, you will gain more awareness on how you can benefit from the following chapters. If you do not yet have a community, assume the score is 1 for every statement.

*If your community has some level of secrecy, due to either the vulnerability of its members (e.g. AA) or its nature (e.g. Fight Club), instead use the statement "People help to preserve the identity of our community."

Scores

9–15: You can do better. Where are the main gaps?

16–22: Way to go! What's the main focus area to make it even better?

23–27: You must be doing something right. What's next?

CONNECTEDNESS Direct connections and ongoing conversations between people.	
Community members are directly in touch with each other.	
There is a place where members can find each other at any time (e.g. an online platform).	
We have recurring points of interaction (i.e. gatherings, whether online or offline).	
IDENTITY Excitement to belong. Being part of the community adds real value to a member's identity.	
There is a clear criteria that defines our community members.	
I trust that people who participate will represent our community well.	
People are glad to share that they are part of our community.*	
GROWTH The community grows organically. Every member represents it and expands the organization's reach.	
Our members constantly invite new people into our community.	
Our members are willing to run activities that help our community grow.	
There is more than one chapter of our community started by one of our members.	
TOTAL SCORE	

The Art of Community Building

Part II In a Nutshell

In Part I, we went through the key principles for community building, gaining a bird's-eye view of the forest. Now we will get down to earth and walk through the trees. In the following chapters, we will go through the practical steps of building or growing a community.

First, we'll understand the development stages of a community, from one to many. Using the principle that communities are organic systems, we will explore a framework called Community Life Cycle, which uses nature as a metaphor for the stages of organic growth.

In Chapter 12, we will use storytelling in a practical way and create a character through a couple of exercises. We will take elements from branding and storytelling, explore famous characters who have stood the test of time and understand what makes them so special. In decoding the secret to their success with a framework called Character Diamond, I will help you better understand yourself and your brand. Following on that thread, in Chapter 13, we will talk about how to translate your core to practice, by using the Community Scorecard framework.

The later chapters will take you through the fundamental steps to building and growing a community. Try to read Chapters 14 to 17 on a streak because these chapters make the most impact when considered together. This section is the key hypothesis of this book and brings community building into practice, in steps that interconnect.

I believe that the essence of community is people sharing (anything). For sharing to happen, there must be trust, which is created through safe spaces where people feel at home to be authentic. A key theme of this book is that we build and enhance trust through encounters and relevance. In Chapter 14, we will talk about bringing people together—both why we must do it and the key elements of designing good reasons to gather. In Chapter 15, we will consider the importance of cadence in enhancing trust and building intimate relationships. We'll look at ways of attracting people to your community and then at the importance of engaging them and encouraging them to commit, using a funnel framework.

In Chapter 16, we will explore the idea of engineering serendipity, which can accelerate the development of relationships within your community by increasing the probability of successful collisions. We will also examine why diversity matters and how to purposefully mix crowds within your community.

Then, in Chapter 17, we will use the Closeness Circles framework to understand how to build and enhance intimacy with people at different levels in your community. This concept goes back to the idea of vulnerability as the fundamental element of authentic communication. The closer people are to your core, the more vulnerably you communicate with each other, and that itself grows trust between you. We will explore how to design such vulnerability-driven communication in your community.

Chapter 18 brings us back to some of the concepts we explored in Part I, including the importance of humility and letting grow. It also builds on the concepts presented in Chapter 17, including how your role as a community builder is to make yourself obsolete and empower others to keep your community growing.

In the final chapter of this book, I remind you that community building is a lifelong journey and explore how vulnerability, self-love and acceptance are key parts of the adventure.

Wishing you a joyful journey through Part II. Let's walk together.

CHAPTER 11

Community Life Cycle: Development Stages

"Never doubt that a small group of thoughtful, committed citizens can change the world. Indeed, it's the only thing that ever has."

—MARGARET MEAD

Community Grows Like Nature Does

A single dandelion head can produce up to 172 seeds, all sharing the same core. Each seed is carried in the wind, spreading across the fields, even growing through cracks in the sidewalk. Each seed can sprout, grow from seed to bud, to become a plant just like the one it originated from. Each flower turns into another seed head made up of another 172 seeds.

While dandelions are the perfect metaphor for organic growth, people also follow organic patterns. And like the first seed is needed to spread dandelions, a founder's core is fundamental to grow a community. Communities are made of people and, as such, are also organic systems.

There is an aspect of fractality to the way communities grow. A single fractal can represent the whole system it belongs to. A fractal is the smallest part of a chaotic system that follows the same pattern as the whole. Each part is a representation of the entire system.

> **fractal**
>
> *noun*
>
> frac·tal
>
> Definition of *fractal*: any of various extremely irregular curves or shapes for which any suitably chosen part is similar in shape to a given larger or smaller part when magnified or reduced to the same size
>
> Source: *Merriam-Webster*

The starting point of a community is generally an individual or a small group: the founding team. A group gathered around a central idea or mission has the potential to grow into a movement that spreads all over the world. As it grows, it spreads its core through each individual. As these core beliefs translate into decisions and actions, the evidence of a community is often in the pattern of behaviors represented by each individual: its culture.

A single company could also start a community. As we've seen in Part I, Swedish startup culture still follows values and principles similar to those used by Lars Magnus Ericsson and Ingvar Kamprad, the founder of IKEA. Similarly, the culture of openness and free exchange of ideas in Silicon Valley dates back to the 1950s. The values here were influenced by the community spread by former employees of the Fairchild Semiconductor Corporation, whose rich family tree includes Intel, Sequoia Capital, Apple, Oracle, Cisco, and more. More recently, the Paypal Mafia also shared core values. The payment solutions business spread its entrepreneurial seeds through its former employees, who eventually went on to start a series of innovative companies such as LinkedIn, Square, YouTube, Yelp, Tesla, and SpaceX.

A founder's core will define the DNA of their community, from how they recruit to how they gather people together. Their actions will influence the people around them and reinforce the main values. A founder's core is made of beliefs and values that steer the decision-making process, define their actions, and influence individual behavior. Collectively speaking, this compound of behaviors driven by group values is what we call culture.

What else can we learn from nature about the organic growth framework?

- **Organic growth starts from a core (seed).**
  In communities, it's just the same. The core (beliefs, purpose, values) of a founder is equivalent to the seed in nature.

- **It grows through cultivation, not through control.**
  There is no centralized management for organic growth, and context matters. If seeds don't settle into the right environment, they won't grow.

- **Organic systems evolve to accomplish multiple and complementary functions, while still representing the core (e.g. cells with different functions but the same DNA).**
  In a community, individuals grow to fulfill different roles while sharing the same values.

The Cycles of Community Development: From You to Thousands

How can you engineer the growth of organic communities? Let's go back to nature. From dandelions to our bodies, nature seems to like following a sequence of numbers in various patterns. We call it the FibonaccI sequence, discovered by Leonardo Pisano, a 13th-century Italian mathematician and the son of Bonacci, or "fils de Bonacci." His findings were based on a study of how rabbits reproduce. While the FibonaccI sequence isn't pervasive everywhere in the natural world, it is found often enough to be impressive. Also known as the golden ratio (or divine proportion), its visual representation is an iconic spiral. Its resemblance to several shapes in nature is uncanny, from the Milky Way, to seashells and succulents.

Now we will use the golden ratio as a metaphor to illustrate the life cycle of a community, from seed to seed ball, from one to thousands. We'll call it the Golden Cycle.

Life Cycle of a Community Overview

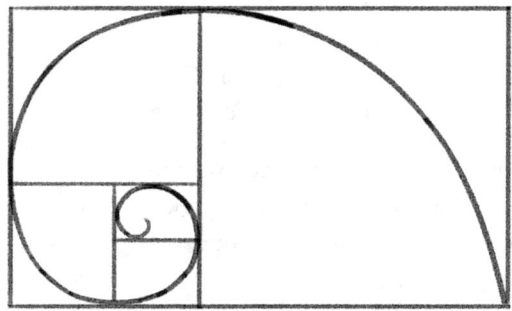

Seed: you define the community core (values, mission, purpose)

Sprout: you reach out and tell your story, communicating your core

Bud: people start to gather around the core

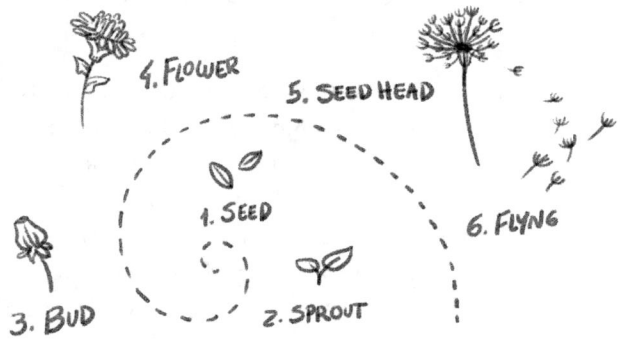

Stage	Action
Seed	Define core (belief, values, mindset), first steps of branding, identity creation and character development.
Sprout	Start speaking, showing up, reaching out, storytelling and overcommunicating your core.
Bud	You attract the first group of people who resonate with your story and share your core. The first ten to one hundred people are crucial.
Flower	The first ones help share your story, attracting the next people. You start creating layers of commitment and roles.
Seed head	As you grow, you develop more complex layers of commitment, enhancing a sense of ownership.
Flying	Empowered members restart the process, repeating what you've done, but this time at scale and under your guidance.

Flower: concrete initiatives form to grow and attract more people

Seed head: you start empowering people to spread your core

Flying: people spread their wings to help expand your community

Getting Started

The following chapters will explore the stages of community development using this model. It is important to remember we are never at one single or fixed stage of development, both because these stages are merely a metaphor for reality—which is imperfect and impermanent—and, more importantly, because when building communities, you are often between two stages.

The more the community grows, the more likely you will find yourself in various stages at once (represented by 1000^n). If you succeed to grow as dandelions do, there will always be new communities that emerge from yours, each growing at a different pace.

First, we will look at the journey from seed to bud, defining your core and crafting your story. Then, from bud to sprout, taking your first step outside to reach out to your first ten to fifty people with your story. Then, we'll go from sprout to flower, creating a more complex system to attract people to your community and engineering serendipity to engage them further. In the next step, from flower to seed head, we will discuss designing layers of commitment to prepare people for flying. Encouraging ownership and creating frameworks will empower them to start new communities that replicate your core.

If you are starting a community from scratch, the steps in the following chapters will walk you through the entire process.

If you aim to grow an existing community, use these frameworks to audit the current state of your community. Doing so will help to validate your core and re-design a growth strategy, enabling you to do more of what you're doing well and to improve in areas where it is needed.

CHAPTER 12

From Seed to Sprout: Finding Your Core

> *"'Who are YOU?' said the Caterpillar.*
> *This was not an encouraging opening for a conversation. Alice replied, rather shyly, 'I—I hardly know, sir, just at present—at least I know who I WAS when I got up this morning, but I think I must have been changed several times since then.'"*
>
> —*ALICE'S ADVENTURES IN WONDERLAND*, LEWIS CARROLL

Who Are You?

Most of us introduce ourselves by stating where we come from, our role in society, what we do for work, our family name, our hometown, our country, or our ethnicity. While these can be defining characteristics of who you are, you are more than this. While you can be patriotic for your country or hometown, you cannot choose your origins. While you can introduce yourself by the roles you have in your family, society, and community, these are temporary.

You are what you show to the world: the good, the bad, and the ugly. However, you are also what you care deeply for, and, more importantly, you are what you make of your journey, as well as what it makes of you. Your journey is made up of your decisions, which are products of your values. Your story includes where you came from and how you got to where you are now. It illustrates your character.

You are who you become along your journey. So tell your story.

In his book *Branding: In Five and a Half Steps*, Michael Johnson helps us find a way forward. "Let's start with the core. Most people in this business agree that a core, central 'idea' is critical," he writes. "In order to define what this can be, it helps to think of it as the core purpose of a company, brand or organization. Start by answering the question 'why are we here?', 'what have we been put upon this earth to do?'. If you can clearly define why you're here, then it makes it a lot easier for people to 'get' what you stand for."

Becoming a Character

> *"It's a dangerous business, Frodo, going out your door. You step onto the road, and if you don't keep your feet, there's no knowing where you might be swept off to."*
>
> —BILBO TO FRODO BAGGINS IN *THE LORD OF THE RINGS*, J.R.R. TOLKIEN

Who is the character before the journey? Picture Dorothy before the cyclone, in Kansas singing "Over the Rainbow." There is longing in her voice. Picture Bilbo Baggins when Gandalf and the Dwarves invade his house and lure him to the Lonely Mountain. There is curiosity, yet refusal to accept the invitation.

As Joseph Campbell explains in *The Hero of a Thousand Faces*, at the beginning of their journey, the hero is in their ordinary world. Dorothy is still at the farm in Kansas. Bilbo is smoking a pipe in the Shire. Then, they receive a call to adventure. Dorothy runs away from home and meets Professor Marvel. Gandalf unexpectedly visits Bilbo's home. The plot continues with a refusal. Dorothy runs back home, trying to protect herself from the cyclone. Bilbo is upset at the twelve Dwarves in his hobbit-hole, finding himself hosting an unexpected party. But in the next step of the Journey, we're no longer in Kansas, nor in the Shire. The hero has embarked on the adventure, and the rest is history.

Now, let's bring it back to the real world.

Think of a young Martin Luther King, Jr. reading the Bible and singing in his church choir. At thirteen, he became the youngest assistant manager of a newspaper delivery station at the *Atlanta Journal*, and the same year he denied the bodily resurrection of Jesus at Sunday School. Later, he began doctoral studies in systematic theology at Boston University, and, at age twenty-five, he became a pastor.

I don't know about you, but reading about this activist's early life sparks me to learn more. In Dr. King's own words, "People think of me as a civil rights leader, but fundamentally, I'm a Baptist preacher." Through his private writings, we can see that while leading from his core of Christian values, Dr. King rejected biblical literalism and criticized the church for perpetuating injustice through practices such as slavery and segregation. His core steered his every step in leading the civil rights movement in his own way, eventually leading him to receive a Nobel Peace Prize and become a historic figure.

We see real-life characters at the end of their journeys. We know them for what they've accomplished. But what makes their accomplishments so impressive is where they started. Where did they come from? What fueled them to act? What event in their lives sparked the first fire that would one day light up the entire world? Who or what gave them the ideas that would enlighten others?

Exercise 1: Find Your Core (20 minutes)

> *"Core values are the deeply ingrained principles that guide all of a company's actions; they serve as its cultural cornerstones."*
>
> —*THE FOUR OBSESSIONS OF AN EXTRAORDINARY EXECUTIVE,* PATRICK LENCIONI

Discovering what moves you is a three-step practice. Before we dive deep, let's dip our toes into the water to feel the temperature. This will guide your next step, walking you closer to your core.

> **Note:** if you're doing these exercises as an existing community or organization, I advise you to do this exercise as individuals first. Then extend the same questions to the organization as a whole.

→ Step 1 (5–10 minutes)

Actions speak louder than words. What you do is based on your values. At its simplest, values define what matters to you, and what you care for.

VALUES > DECISIONS > ACTIONS

Before we get to the nitty-gritty questions to identify your values, let's take a look at your emotions. Emotions fuel your actions.

Instructions:

Jot down the answers to the following questions, thinking back to relevant moments in your life.

1. What gets you angry?

2. What makes you afraid?

3. What makes you sad?

4. What gets you excited?

5. What evokes tears of joy?

Journal about each question for at least one minute without stopping. Even if nothing comes to mind, write gibberish. Like *"I don't know what I am writing about, what gets me angry?"* or whatever comes out. Write until a story comes to mind.

Then, take a moment to read what you just wrote. Think back at those moments you felt angry, thrilled, or touched. What do these moments mean to you?

Outcome

What makes you angry reveals something about what you value. For example, I felt angry when a group of teenagers cut in line for a taxI in front of a heavily pregnant woman. She'd been standing behind me, and had declined my offer for her to go in front of me. When the teenagers showed up and tried to pass ahead of us, I felt that Quentin Tarantino kind of rage emerging through me. In the end, I didn't act on this rage, but I did learn more about myself.

Anger gives voice to the values we hold deep inside. In my example, I heard that kindness towards others, justice, and social responsibility are important to me. I learned that I value helping each other first, instead of acting according to your own interests.

You can examine other emotions in the same way. For example, I get teary-eyed watching movies about people overcoming challenges, from *The Shawshank Redemption* to *Invictus*, and perhaps other films starring Morgan Freeman. This reveals that I am moved by people overcoming obstacles and that I find such actions admirable and inspiring. Where else have you caught emotion surfacing?

➡ **Step 2** (5–10 minutes)

It's best to do this exercise with another person. Find a bunch of Post-it notes, a large piece of paper, a pen, and let's roll with it.

Instructions:

Replicate the following diagram with the numbers 1–5 across the top on a piece of paper.

Set it aside

```
                    WHY ?

        1  →  2  →  3  →  4  →  5
```

1. Grab your pen and sticky notes. Start by answering the question "What brings you to life?" You can think of it as, "What would you, your surroundings, and the world be like if you achieved what you aim to?"

Set a timer for one minute.

    a. Write one sentence per sticky note.

    b. Scribble on as many sticky notes as you want.

    c. Stick the notes randomly on the paper before you.

    d. Keep it under one minute.

2. Stop. Sit back. Breathe, take a sip of coffee, water, or tea. Now, read each statement one by one and let it sink in.

   a. Which sounds most like your daily to-do list, actions, and how you work?

   b. Which sounds closer to what defines your decision-making process (core values) and to the impact you aim to make (vision and goals)?

The closer a statement gets to your core, the closer it is to the "effect" side. The closer it is to what influences big decisions, the more likely it is that you are talking about values—it drives you closer to the impact you want to generate, and also closer to the "effect" side. The closer it is to your actions, daily tasks and *modus operandi*, the more likely it is a cause.

Now, reorder them based on cause and effect:

   a. The closer to 1, the closer to cause, to the "what you do."

   b. The closer to 5, the closer to the effect, to the "why you do it."

3. Alternatively, you can also do this exercise by picking the one that feels closest to your core and ask why for five rounds. You can rephrase it as "Why does it matter? Why is it important? Why do you care about this?"

Scribble down your answer on the sticky notes, one round at a time. Repeat the process at least five times, or until you feel that it is important "because it just is."

   a. Write one or two sentences per sticky note.

   b. Feel free to scribble on as many sticky notes each time you ask why.

   c. Stick the notes randomly on the paper before you and reorder it.

....

Example

First round:

Sample of statements in answer to the question "Why are you here?"

    1. People should feel safe to express themselves.

    2. Happier people lead a kinder world.

    3. When people feel safe, they are more likely to help others.

    4. Kindness generates kindness.

    5. Leaders should host spaces for people to be the best versions of themselves.

Second round:

Reordered responses based on the statements above (1= cause and 5 = effect)

    1. Leaders should host spaces for people to be the best versions of themselves.

    2. People should feel safe to express themselves.

    3. When people feel safe, they are more likely to help others.

    4. Kindness generates kindness.

    5. Happier people lead a kinder world.

Third (optional) round:

Going deeper, asking five times "why" and starting from the one which sounds closest to the "why."

    1. Happier people lead a kinder world. **Why does it matter?**

    2. Because kindness makes people feel cared for. **Why does it matter?**

    3. When we feel we are cared for, they care for others. **Why does it matter?**

4. When people feel cared for, they live longer and better lives.
Why does it matter?

5. For people to live better lives.

....

At the end of the exercise, you'll get to a statement where you can no longer keep answering "why?" It gets to the point where it is important "because it just is." On the way to this point, you'll discover several statements that could become part of your manifesto. But the one that matters the most is the very last one after asking five rounds of "why?" and reorganizing.

This is your ultimate vision.

→ Step 3 (5 minutes)

I hope Step 2 helped you gain clarity on what matters to you most and how you work towards it. Both exercises help define your core. I hope you use these insights in your life. We'll also use them in the next chapter, when we discuss storytelling.

Now, think of the community you are building and answer the questions below, which are taken from Michel Johnson's book *Branding: In Five and a Half Steps*.

1. What is the problem we're here to fix?

2. Why does that matter, and why now?

3. What are we doing about it?

4. What do we want others to do?

Take some time to review the output of these exercises and utilize them in any format that helps remind you of your own core. This could evolve into an image that communicates your core or even a manifesto.

Character Development:
The Journey to Becoming More Like You

Let's bring it back to you. What is your story? What events in your life have helped define your beliefs? What grounded your decisions? What is your calling? How are you reacting to it? Whether you are talking about yourself as an individual or an organization building a community, it is the same process. Creating yourself a character will help you communicate it to the world.

Dorothy from *The Wonderful Wizard of Oz* isn't a one-book character. She's also Alice from *Alice's Adventures in Wonderland* and Belle from *Beauty and the Beast*. They are the same character. Besides singing in white blouses underneath blue dresses, what do they all have in common?

The willingness to explore somewhere beyond their own world. A journey into an unknown land where they'll redefine their preconceived notions of reality. Perhaps including an enchanted castle where utensils sing. In the Disney version of *Alice in Wonderland*, Alice sings about being in a world of her own. Dorothy wonders "If birds fly over the rainbow / Oh why, oh why can't I?" and Belle sings "I want much more than this provincial life / I want adventures in the great wide somewhere." In *The Sound of Music*, Maria shares a very similar journey and we hear her belting, "The hills fill my heart with the sound of music / My heart wants to sing every song it hears." She even fashions the same kind of dress.

But isn't this type of longing common in every character? Not quite.

There are characters we all know through different names. Look at Sherlock Holmes, Dr. House, and Harvey Specter from *Suits*. Brilliant, yet arrogant. Necessary, yet unsuitable to their societies. Misunderstood geniuses who can't fit in and cope with the help of some sort of substance abuse. Besides that, they are all great helpers of humanity.

How do creators create such contagious characters, who persist through time and keep enchanting us, from start to finish, with the same old stories? And how does this help you? It is time to build yourself a contagious character.

Exercise 2: The Character Diamond

This is a framework to get you started on showing up and sharing your story with the world. I learned it from Roy Williams, founder and president of the Wizard Academy, a nontraditional business school that helps a wide variety of businesses do consciously what gifted people do unconsciously.

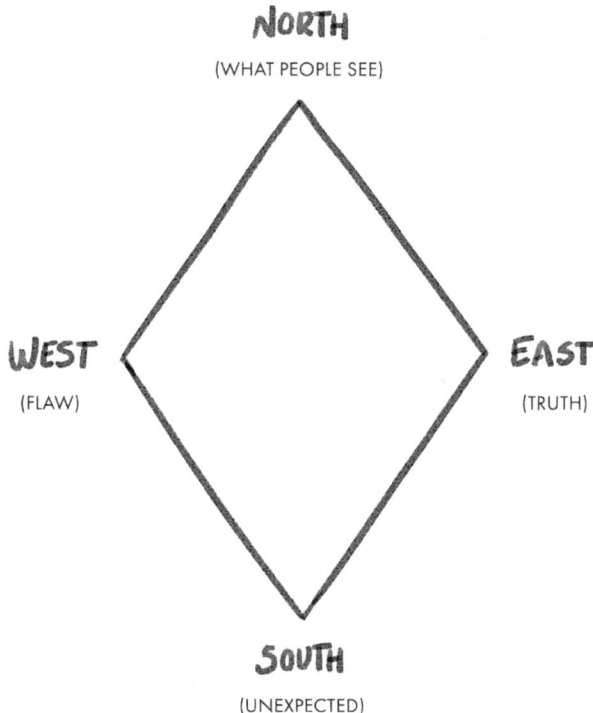

Good characters are not obvious—in fact, they are rather complex. Sometimes they make no sense. They might even upset us, yet we keep rooting for them. Why is this?

Instructions:

Think of one of your favorite characters and consider the following:

North: Stereotype. What people see first. The stereotypical face of the person.

South: Contradiction. Something that breaks the expectations from the north stereotype.

West: Flaw. Something that plays against them. A vulnerability.

East: Core. Something close to their hearts that speaks to their utmost truth.

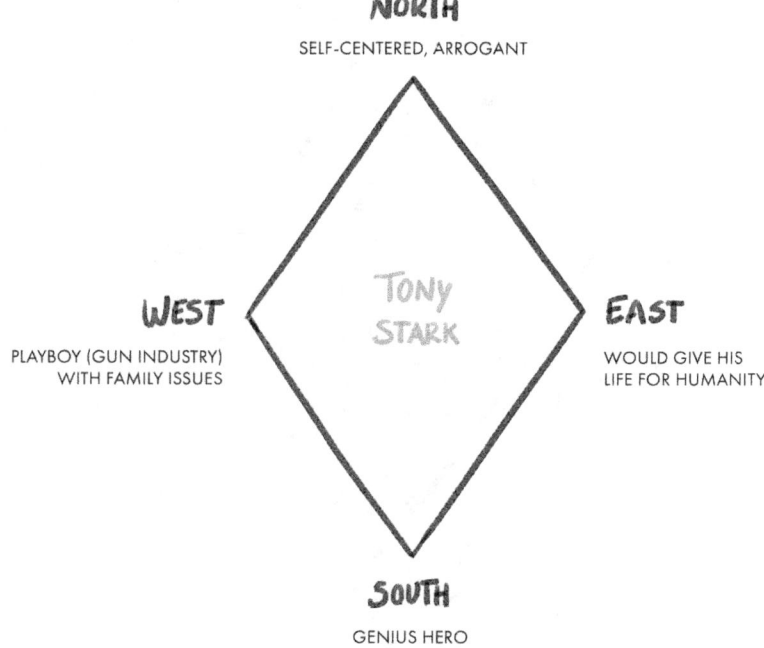

I'll use the example of Iron Man himself, Tony Stark. He reveals himself to be a self-centered, arrogant businessman, who, wait… happens to be an absolute genius and uses his abilities to save the world. That is not what we expect from an entitled rich guy. Even less when he's the only child of an arms dealer. Tony Stark is full of flaws and contradictions. He acts out like a spoiled playboy and often disrespects people. He hides family issues with his father. He feels like an absolute failure. He actually cares for humanity.

Against the odds, this "genius, billionaire, playboy philanthropist," as he refers to himself, would actually give his life to save the world.

The North-South axis is about what is visible on the surface. Because there are contradictory aspects at play here, we give it attention. Why? Our brains like to save time. We tend to predict likely outcomes and relax, unless something unexpected happens. The goal of contradiction is to create that unexpected element that catches our eye. Now, we're paying attention. What happens next?

The West-East axis is about what's underneath the surface. This is where we relate to characters. Your flaws are in the West. Sharing these—thoughtfully and tastefully—allows people to connect to you in a real and authentic way. In the East are your ultimate goals, purposes, and values. The West-East composition is what makes you real. These are your flaws and what you deeply care about. It is what makes a character human.

Now, take five minutes to draft your own character diamond, and that of your community.

Make Your Flaws Your Strength

> *"There is a crack in everything*
> *That's how the light gets in"*
>
> —"ANTHEM," LEONARD COHEN

No one can relate to perfection. Flaws show that we're human. As Robin Roberts says, "make your mess your message." I'll share two stories to show the advantages of sharing your flaws. The first is a classic branding example from Avis, the car rental company.

In *Branding: In Five and a Half Steps*, Michael Johnson says:

> ...sometimes the real "truth" is harder to acknowledge. In the early 1960s an agency team toiled over what the car rental company Avis truly offered to the world. Its researchers kept coming back with the same phrase: "We try harder because we have to." There was little else to differentiate Avis from Hertz, the market leader, or the other rental brands. This research insight led to one of the finest copy lines of the last 50 years: "Avis is only no. 2... We try harder." This honesty carried over into the headlines—"Avis can't afford not to be nice," "Avis can't afford dirty ashtrays," "Avis can't afford to make you wait." The durability of the insight and the quality of the work continued for decades.

He says that they updated their slogan in 2012, but soon returned to "We try harder" sixty years after it was first used. Why? According to Johnson, "because it doesn't pretend to be something it's not (Avis isn't pitching to the world's biggest or best). It has warmth, humility, is based in a product 'truth,' it is 'defensible' (i.e. hard for others to adopt) and helps Avis stand out in a tricky and competitive market."

The second example is a personal story.

In 2013, while in Argentina, I got my first startup experience at an educational startup, where I helped organize the first one hundred percent online conference of its kind.

We had eighty-five sought-after speakers and experts from across the Latin America startup ecosystem. We sold thousands of tickets to people from all across Latin America. The event had been especially popular in countries with less-developed startup ecosystems, such as Dominican Republic and Ecuador.

Note that at the time, online conferences didn't exist like they do today. Back then, our conference technology was not bulletproof and we faced a major system crash on the first day of the event. Our users were frustrated. Angry emails and Facebook messages poured in by the minute. My team was devastated. One of the founders was ready to burst into tears. I was ashamed. I considered walking away for a minute.

This was the founders' responsibility, or it was the CTO's role to fix it. But that didn't solve my shame problem, nor did it alleviate the problem thousands of frustrated customers faced.

I noticed that the angriest users were the ones who cared the most. I suggested that we should write our customers a letter immediately, apologizing and admitting we screwed up, and saying that although we did not yet know how, we would fix it and deliver our promise within a day. If they wanted their money back, they could have it. However, if they could forgive our technical failure and wait just a day, we would make it up and they'd still get the experience they were promised. So that's what we did—we admitted our mistake and apologized.

A great majority stayed and sent us notes of support.

That night, we worked until 5 am, when we implemented our solution. We would spread the content across three weeks, releasing the burden from our overwhelmed servers that couldn't support so many users at once.

The next thing we knew, founders and aspiring entrepreneurs from all over Latin America were discussing Bitcoin with the legendary Wenceslao Casares, an Argentinean entrepreneur who founded and sat on the boards of numerous big ventures. Previously, he had only been accessible to entrepreneurs in big cities like Buenos Aires

It was worth it.

Our community only stayed with us after we showed vulnerability. We admitted our mistakes, while reminding them that we deeply cared and wanted to deliver the experience, knowledge, and networks we had promised. We created a stronger community from our mistake.

CHAPTER 13

From Sprout to Bud: Building Belonging through Relatable Stories

"We cannot teach people anything; we can only help them discover it within themselves."

—GALILEO GALILEI

Telling Stories that Bring People Together

A brand is communication of values. It's not about you, but about the value your brand can provide to people. So let's craft a story that shares your core in a way that your soon-to-be community can relate to.

Our goal is to communicate to the world why we exist in the most conducive ways. You can do this through a brand manifesto or by creating an image that speaks a thousand words. It can be anything that resonates with others, as if reminding them of something they already knew. We only resonate with a story when it speaks to something we already feel at heart. As Simon Sinek put it in his TED talk "How great leaders inspire action," your goal is to reach out to people who believe what you believe.

SHARED BELIEF > VALUES > DECISIONS > ACTIONS

↓

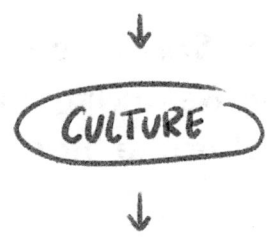

↓

FEWER DOLLARS SPENT
ADVERTISING, MANAGEMENT, RECRUITING

There is more to a brand than the colors, words, and fonts we choose to promote our company. Quoting Michael Johnson, "If we asked 'what makes up Virgin's brand?' we'd be balancing a whole basket of values, behaviours, the principle of 'challenging in markets,' the irrepressible personality of its bearded founder—and the way the logo appears on planes, trains, and credit cards."

Creating culture is fundamental to creating a brand. It is about building a strong leadership team, as well as creating, reinforcing and over-communicating clarity. Yes, over-communication is a strategic part of spreading your core. In a nutshell, you must empower people to spread your core as you build a sense of ownership.

Creating a Community Scorecard

A Community Scorecard is a cause-and-effect map, a hybrid creation inspired by the Balance Scorecard, the Business Model Canvas, and Simon Sinek's Golden Circle. This framework will help you define:

- Why you exist: your purpose
- How you go about achieving your purpose: your mission statement
- How you make your purpose real: your actions, products, and tasks
- What resources you need to make it real: concrete support to make it viable
- Who shares your journey: the people who can join you from the start

This process can also help you define your measurements of success.

Exercise: Community Scorecard

Creating this can be made easier if you've already worked on cause and effect statements in the previous chapter. To explain how the Community Scorecard works, let's use the example statement we arrived at at the end of the Find Your Core exercise: **For people to live better lives.**

Instructions

Replicate the table below on a piece of paper.

Why	Vision	
How	Mission	
What	Key Activities (enablers)	
	Key Resources (supporters)	
	Key Partners	

Fill out the table using your mission. Here's a version using the example from the previous chapter: *For people to live better lives.*

1. **Vision:** Describe your ultimate vision, your goal, the "why you are doing it."

    Example: For people to live better lives.

2. **Mission:** The way you work towards your goal, the "how you will do it."

   Example: By multiplying safe spaces where people truly belong

3. **Key Activities (enablers):** List the concrete "to dos" needed to accomplish your mission, the "what you do."

   Example:

   a. Sharing knowledge about community building (book, courses)

   b. Developing community leaders through programs

   c. Consulting for community development around the world

4. **Key Resources (supporters):** List the material aspects that are required to achieve your goal (talent, knowledge, capital, etc).

   Example:

   a. Time (to write a book)

   b. Platform (to share knowledge)

   c. Team

5. **Key Partners:** Write down the people and organizations that can help you accomplish your mission through shared resources or activities.

   Example:

   a. Seasoned and knowledgeable community leaders

   b. Organizations that provide community-building services

Crafting Measurements of Success

Three types of measures can be intuitively extracted from your vision, mission, and key activities. All of these must be concrete enough to be verifiable over time and help you track the success of your community-building efforts.

- **Measurements of Success (MoS):** Generally closer to the mission and vision, these are the numbers you will use when determining your biggest impact.
- **Milestones:** These are not numerical, but concrete and verifiable events that represent how you've accomplished a key part of the journey towards your goals.
- **Key Performance Indicators (KPIs):** These are numbers that indicate you are on track to reach your goals. They're essentially benchmarks of what you have accomplished.

These measurements align with the Community Scorecard:

- The closer to the top of the Community Scorecard (mission, vision): MoS.
- From middle to bottom (Key Activities, Key Resources, and Key Partners): Milestone or KPI, both of which can indicate how well you are performing to reach your bigger goals.

Let's apply our example to show how this works.

Community Scorecard Section		Measurement	Type
Vision	For people to live better lives.	Number of lives touched (people in communities)	MoS
Mission	To multiply safe spaces where people truly belong	Number of communities started	MoS
Key Activities	Sharing knowledge on community building (through a book, courses)	Book written and courses launched	Milestone
	Developing community leaders through programs	Number of program batches	KPI
		Number of community leaders developed	KPI
	Consulting for community development around the world	Number of communities reached	KPI

Building an Authentic Brand

Start from feeling at home with yourself. Then, create a safe space and share it with others. Create a place that feels like home for them as well.

Depart from your core, make decisions that resonate with your heart, and most likely everything you say and do will resemble you. Get to know yourself and acknowledge it may be a long ride. It's not about reaching a million followers, but more about who you become on your way there. The relationships you create, the friends you make, and the experiences you have are what help you become more authentic.

Communicate who you are, your values and your message, in a way that truly, authentically honors you and your brand purpose, not who you think you should be or what others say.

We Need to Reinvent Stories

> *"As we let our own light shine, we unconsciously give other people permission to do the same."*
>
> —NELSON MANDELA

You need a strong story as a community, as an individual, and as an organization. From the moment you create a character, you're no longer alone and can better communicate yourself and your core to the world. In doing so, you allow others to enter your space.

Powerful stories are those we can relate with. I feel comfortable speaking about Dorothy, Alice, Belle, and Maria because I can relate to each of them. However, we often have to be careful which stories we relate to and why. Some stories speak of values and norms that have become outdated in society or are no longer accurate. While some of those stories helped me grow as an individual and build relationships, I am also aware the underlying message or values may now belong to the past. We need to take another look at traditions that may no longer be constructive in the current world. We must reinvent stories that make more sense for the current reality, that drive progress in the right direction.

For example, we need to embed diversity, tolerance, and equality in our communities. To create more diverse communities, we need more diverse leaders. For people to rise, they need positive stories of people who resemble them making a stand. Representation and resonance have an effective, lasting impact on communities. While we can still improve, contemporary leadership boards are starting to reflect our communities more accurately than they used to.

Having an appropriate example can inspire and motivate others. For example, Roger Bannister set a precedent that empowered other athletes to push beyond what many thought was impossible. Bill Taylor explains in an article for *Harvard Business Review*, "When Bannister broke the mark, even his most ardent rivals breathed a sigh of relief. At last, somebody did it! And once they saw it could be done, they did it too. Just 46 days after Bannister's feat, John Landy, an Australian runner, not only broke the barrier again, with a time of 3 minutes 58 seconds. Then, just a year later, three runners broke the four-minute barrier in a single race. Over the last half century, more than a thousand runners have conquered a barrier that had once been considered hopelessly out of reach."

Sharing stories can shift the vision of what we believe is possible. Wharton professors Yoram Wind and Colin Crook explain the four-minute mile effect. In their book, *The Power of Impossible Thinking*, they say that it was not a "genetic engineering experiment that created a new race of super runners," nor a "sudden growth spurt in human evolution." Rather, it was a matter of mindset. They explain, "The runners of the past had been held back by a mindset that said they could not surpass the four-minute mile. When that limit was broken, the others saw that they could do something they had previously thought impossible."

During my time at Startup Genome, I had the opportunity to visit Helsinki, which is a rising star amongst startup ecosystems. In order to decode its success, I interviewed a few key players, from founders to community builders and investors. AnssI Rantanen, a Helsinki-based entrepreneur and director of European educational company Growth Tribe, revealed that the entrepreneurship path is clear in Finland. His path as an entrepreneur became clear for him after hearing success stories from peers of similar age, a concept I call "accessible success stories."

These stories were not about how seasoned entrepreneurs sold their companies for a billion dollars, but examples such as how another student participated in one of the earliest startup accelerator programs, Startup Sauna, then raised six-figure seed capital to pursue his business. AnssI resonated with this story because he could see that success was attainable. He believed it was possible for himself and was inspired by his successful peers to take the first steps. Stories create possibilities. The moment you see someone who resembles you attaining the seemingly impossible, success is no longer a far-fetched theory, but a possibility. We need to reinvent stories that make more sense for now and future generations. We need to tell stories that have diversity and equality embedded in them, in order to inspire and encourage further diversity.

CHAPTER 14

From Bud to Flower: Bringing People Together

"A real conversation always contains an invitation. You are inviting another person to reveal herself or himself to you, to tell you who they are or what they want."

—DAVID WHYTE

Creating Excuses to Bring People Together

In truth, there is no such thing as community building. Some people already belong together. A community builder's role is simply to connect them.

Bringing people together is the first step towards connectedness. But building a community means taking a step further to make sure that these people *stay* connected. Your role is to bring people together consistently enough to grow a sense of familiarity among them.

The more we see each other, the more we talk, the more we connect, and the more we trust. Building communities is like building collective relationships.

To build closeness and intimacy, people need time and space to interact, build familiarity and create authentic connections. This is probably why many of us have close friends who we met at school, in the neighborhood, or at work. It's not about the activity we perform together (attending classes, neighborhood parties, or shared projects), but about spending enough time together to build bonds. What brings us together isn't necessarily what binds us together.

On that note, I love the definition from a friend of mine: that "community building is hosting parties with a purpose." This is true as long as your parties are consistent to your core, follow a reliable cadence and stay cohesive over time.

The goal is getting people to interact consistently enough to build authentic relationships.

From this chapter onwards, we will talk about how to bring people together: a first step. This includes:

1. Designing good "excuses" to bring people together

2. Respecting the three Cs of connectedness: consistency, cadence, and cohesion

3. Building relationships through content design: attract, engage, commit

4. Engineering serendipity: enhancing the likelihood of successful connections

5. Building closeness and empowering people within your community

There is a lot in common between Hugh Mason's turkey and the "watercooler effect" analogy. However, as we will see in the next chapter, not every collision will be successful, but the more collisions, the more likely a connection will happen.

Bringing People Together Around MEALs

Going forward, I will refer to anything we do to bring people together as the MEAL. Why? First, to honor food as the most ancient element that brings people together. Second, to illustrate how anything could bring people together. If I use the term "event" dinners, parties, and webinars come to mind.

If I use "content" you'll think of an article, video, or social media post. In fact, we do need all these, so I'll use MEAL as shorthand to outline a variety of things to bring people together.

Miscellaneous: Anything you can't fit in the three categories below. People just need an excuse to get together. What matters most are the conversations around the table.

Entertainment: Gather together around something light and fun. Anything entertaining, such as sports, movies, music concerts, theater, book clubs, dining, exploring the city for new cocktail bars or a photo safari. Anything!

Action: Invite people to take action together. It could be work-related (a workshop or project), sharing knowledge (a fireside chat or conference), testing a product or service (connecting to a brand), or even planting a tree.

Location: Bringing people to a physical space. It could be driven by a curiosity to see a monument, landscape, or historical building, or it could just be a trip to the watercooler. Your goal is to make it a destination, increasing foot traffic and collision rate, which we will discuss in the next chapter.

MEAL could refer to anything you do that sets a context for conversations, be it a product launch or a dinner party. From grabbing coffee, having a party, or discussing the future of work, it refers to credible and concrete situations that attract people to a common place, physical or virtual. It should also be consistent to your core and simple to replicate. It is fundamental to both keep cadence (recurring encounters) and cohesion (alignment across every MEAL).

When you host a MEAL, you will attract a crowd of **self-selected individuals** who define themselves as members. One single community can host several MEALs. For example, Hubud, the coworking hub in Ubud, Bali, has several elements to attract people, engage them, and encourage commitment to the space. From its Instagrammable bamboo architecture to its healthy food cafe or the uniquely creative and diverse crowd. The self-selected attendees are proud to be part of an innovative digital nomad community of entrepreneurs. Your goal is to organize your MEALs to get people attracted, engaged, and committed to your community.

The Three Cs of Connectedness: Consistency, Cadence, and Cohesion

Connection is not about randomly walking into people. It is about starting a conversation to find that we share something deeper and staying in touch beyond the initial conversation. To engineer authentic connections, three elements must be present in every MEAL: consistency, cadence, and cohesion.

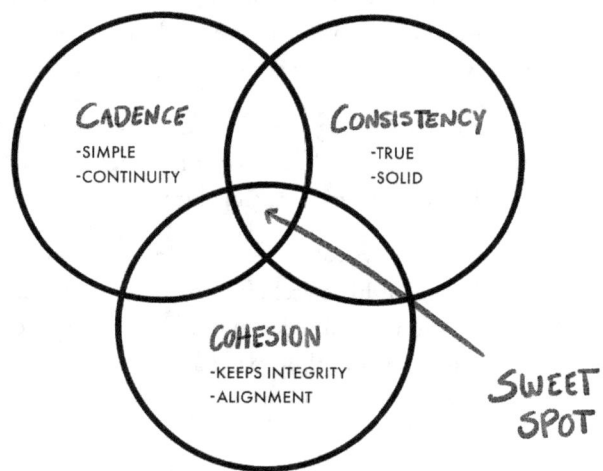

Consistency

Everything you do to bring people together must relate to your core.

When you stand strong in your core, everything you say and do resembles you. Consistency means your core permeates everything you do, from the words you choose in your communication with your crowd, to the people you hold hands with, to the clients you successfully book. Consistency is when everything you say and do is aligned, because your decisions are guided by your core values.

Lack of consistency is like saying, "I am vegan, but I eat fish once in a while." If you were part of a community priding itself on pursuing a fully plant-based lifestyle, how would they react to this? To represent a community identity, you must stay consistent with the same values.

Cadence

Keep it simple and make it replicable.

You meet someone at a party, have a great time with them, but never text or call after. Will this person become your friend? No, right? There is no relationship building without cadence. The more people see each other, the more trust and familiarity organically grow. In order to build trust, you must be reliable. Set clear expectations on communication channels, format, and frequency. As you get to know your community better, design content to attract and engage them with a clear frequency. Your community should know when to expect to hear from you.

Cohesion

Everything you say and do is connected with the past and future. Always stay true to your promises.

Cohesion is the result of your unwavering commitment to make sure your values resound throughout your business. If people sign up to your weekly newsletter and you start spamming them with sales and ads, there's a good chance your messages will be marked as spam and blacklisted by your email provider. Deliver what you promised. Long-term cohesion builds trust and loyalty with the right people who will help you grow organically. If you want to grow from one to one thousand, avoid any deals or shortcuts that may compromise your brand. Instead, dedicate yourself to making hard decisions that take you further, not just faster. If you're building a community from scratch, start with a niche MEAL to attract core members. Start strong and stay cohesive.

Now, tie it all together. Speak from your core to your crowd, talk to them regularly, stay congruent in your decisions. Make friends with those who represent your core values. Give first, and keep showing up and speaking up. The more share your purpose, the more your message grows. Let your community speak up for your brand as well.

Community Mapping: Make Friends Towards the First Fifty

Building a community from scratch is like hosting a house party after just moving to a new city where you don't know anyone. You'll face some challenges gathering people.

After landing in a new city, I advise you explore a bit before hosting a housewarming party. While you get settled building yourself a home, step out and get to know the city. Discover places that feel good. On the way, your choices will lead you to meet people you resonate with, and these people may lead you in the right direction.

Let's say you're the kind of person who is into beer. You're brand new in town, and you might walk into some Irish pubs and meet others who value the classics like you. Then, you might visit some craft breweries, where you find others who also like new adventures in beer. You might find one or two places you particularly like, and as you go back again and again, you might start to get to know the servers or the brewers, be offered tastes of new beers, and meet other regulars. One day, you may find that there are enough beer lovers in town to host a series of cozy gatherings where connoisseurs from different bars and breweries agree to host and share their impressions with a small group. Each event has its own flavor and attracts a different crowd, yet everyone shares the love for a good beer. At the end of each get-together, people stay on for yet another toast. At first, there may be clear divisions between those who prefer an IPA and those who are only into sours, but over time, you might find some of them opening up to new things and trying each other's beer.

Next thing you know, you're hosting the third annual beer festival in your town, with ten thousand attendees and two hundred exhibitors from across the country, all organized by you and your fifty best friends, who you met through those early gatherings.

The example of moving to a new city has clear parallels with starting a community from scratch. But if you are already immersed in a community where you know everyone, you are one step ahead. What matters is to make sure you have some understanding of your community before building a product or hosting an event.

> *"Make friends, not contacts."*
>
> —ONE OF THE STARTUP GRIND VALUES,
> AS DEFINED BY FOUNDER DEREK ANDERSEN

When starting a community from scratch, picture yourself as the foreigner who just arrived in a new city and do your homework:

1. While building a home (finding your core, crafting your story), go out and explore around town.

2. Choose relevant places (communication channels and platforms) that resonate with you.

3. Honor the elderly or peers: respect any existing key players, influencers, or community builders or members in the area (meet and learn from them).

4. Make friends, not contacts. Give first. Figure out where you can add value and start taking action to do so.

In the process, dive deeper into your own mission by aligning it with the greater context. Examine the problem you are here to fix.

1. Who else is currently addressing this problem?

2. How are they currently solving the same problem?

3. If you did not exist, how else would people solve this problem?

Add your findings to a new list or spreadsheet (you can create one or get a template from <u>hackingcommunities.com</u>). Write down the names of people, places, and products that are related to your core, solve a similar problem, or share the same ideals for life. They could become friends, partners, or speakers in the future.

Sometimes making friends with others who have set out to solve the same problem can be beneficial. I learned this first-hand when I built 8Spaces as the online marketplace for flexible workspaces in Malaysia. It was one of the first in Southeast Asia, and soon after starting, competitors started to pop up with similar offerings. Business as usual. At first, I was mad at the competition—this time it was about business, not community. But soon, I came to realize that my competitors were doing two things: making me work at my best, and trying to solve the very problem I was passionate about solving. They actually made my entrepreneurial journey more exciting.

Essentially, my business was seeking solutions to quality of life in the workplace by offering a wide range of more flexible, collaborative spaces. If my competitors managed to solve it better or faster than me, we all still won. Moreover, the Southeast Asian market was big enough for all of us. We collectively pushed an obsolete commercial real estate industry to update itself by innovating and optimizing spaces that were not originally meant for work.

In time, my business was acquired by my largest competitor, thanks to whom my business and efforts have been thriving across Southeast Asia since 2016. That's what matters most.

What kind of connections and conversations are you cultivating?

Rather than competing, befriend the people you admire in your space.
Focus on giving first. Build authentic connections with those who share your core. Cultivating a good community gives people a strong reason to stick with you. They also gain value from connecting with others, in addition to the solution you offer. It might mean turning down deals that may bring good money, but not serve you in the long run nor create the right relationships. Who you collaborate with speaks to who you are and your community. This includes who you hire, who you partner with, and who you choose as your clients.

There might be greater value in your community than in your product or service.

CHAPTER 15

From Flower to Seed Head: Attract, Engage, Commit

"I believe in the purpose of everything living:
That taking is but the forerunner of giving;
That strangers are friends that we some day may meet"

—"FAITH," EDGAR A. GUEST

Building Relationships

We often start conversations from the "what." What do you do? What is your name? Where (or what place) are you from? And as we've seen, "what" brings us together but it doesn't matter as much as "why" we stay together.

In Chapter 14, we discussed how we only need excuses to get together. Conversations around the table enable us to discover we share more than a superficial affinity: we share the same core. In certain circumstances, you might meet someone and feel instantly connected to them. The higher the level of relevance of the context, the more likely it is to happen.

For example, people at a yoga retreat are more likely open to connecting. You are more likely to instantly connect with someone there because you both share an affinity towards the practice, but also because the type of practice itself talks about opening up to vulnerability and connection with others. It might also mean you're in a similar or relatable place in life with others who choose to attend such events.

That high level of significance defined by the context is what I call relevance. Higher relevance contexts tend to lead to faster connections between people.

Regardless of how you first meet a person, you become friends with them by staying in touch. You can't build a relationship without continuing the conversation. Staying connected is fundamental to making friends and building relationships.

As a community builder, it is your responsibility to keep a cadence of encounters that remain consistent and cohesive to your core. Here is a framework to help you plan it.

Lighthouse, Port, City

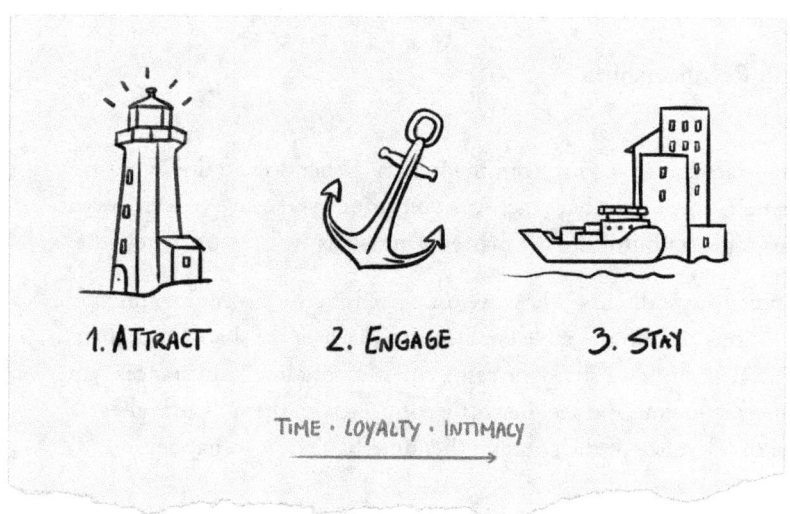

There are different stages to connection:

1. What first brings you to meet someone (like a conversation starter)

2. What brings you to meet again and more often

3. What brings you to stay connected and commit to staying close in a relationship (as friends, partners, fellows, etc.)

In order to deepen connections at a scalable level, I crafted this simple funnel framework to help me design and organize anything I do to bring people together, according to their stage of connection. It divides the MEALs by stage: Attraction, Engagement, and Commitment. We could explain it with a metaphor about how we meet, engage with, and commit to people in real life (such as flirting, dating, then staying together in a relationship), thinking of what types of activities and actions bring us together at these different stages.

For a broader explanation, I prefer using the metaphors of Lighthouse, Port, and City:

1. **Lighthouse.** Like a beacon that guides ships at sea, here your goal is to attract and to become a reference within your cause, industry, or area of impact. Here, you'd generally create MEALs (digital content, products, or events) that cater to a wide audience but that still relate to your core. Lighthouse content, events, or products are often your first interaction with most of your community, playing a key role in building a brand.

Examples: Large music festivals (Coachella), massive boot camps (hackathons) or industry-broad conferences (Web Summit). These events attract a wide range of people who share a similar interest at different levels, from curious to hardcore. They tend to attract hundreds to thousands of individuals, who might not all feel instantly connected to your core. The purpose of this stage is to attract people and lead a high percentage of them to the next stage, the Port, where they will be engaged and find reasons to come back.

2. **Port.** A place people often return to. We might come back to a port for different reasons than the initial attraction that got us there. The purpose of this stage is to build engagement through MEALs that bring people closer to your core. It is all about getting to know each other better and deeper.

Over time, we start to notice people we've seen before and begin to feel familiar with the place. We create memories around it, greet those who used to be strangers, have more intimate conversations, and start to feel like we belong there.

Examples: Hosting private dinners for hardcore people who attended previous events, sending recurring updates to people who signed up to a product (built-in notifications or newsletters), sharing a calendar of future workshops or events that further curate and narrow down interests to connect a niche audience. This stage is all about engagement: you're giving people recurring reasons to come back until they feel like they belong. The purpose is to build relationships with people who share your core the most, building closeness over time until it turns into belonging.

3. **City.** A place where people live, where they are in touch with a wide world of opportunities and people who make them feel at home. This stage is about commitment: it's when people decide to stay and play an active role in your community, becoming a key part of it. Attracted by a lighthouse, we found reasons to come back to a port where we met interesting people and places that felt good. Over time, we built close relationships and memories that made us feel like we belong. We went beyond the port, deeper into a city. We felt at home and decided to stay.

Examples: Building some sort of commitment between people and your community, like when returning customers become brand ambassadors, or your most active member becomes part of your core team. It is about creating roles for active people to hop in and making space for them to take responsibility and be part of growing your community, beyond merely participating in it. The goal of this stage is to multiply your potential to grow your community through these committed members. By trusting them, delegating roles, and empowering them with knowledge and tools, they can fly out, spread the word, and help you grow. It is important to note that, at this stage, you must keep building close relationships with those whom you trust most, on a reciprocal basis.

Staying Cohesive Across all Stages

Even if people are not aware that you're doing it, you must align everything you say and do to your core. Every step you take and every move you make, they'll be watching you. Align every word, every action, every piece of content with the core sentiment.

Sometimes our "why" is too deep to explain in a few words when you want to start attracting people. Start with curiosity and affinity. As you grow closer, you can share more and include them in the process. Finally, they'll start to feel ownership and become part of it.

I often find people who start communities get stuck in the attraction stage. They continue organizing lighthouse-like activities to attract a large crowd, without connecting them through more intimate spaces (other events, smaller gatherings, or online platforms).

Think of building communities as dating. First, you are attracted to someone. It's maybe just about their looks, or because they're wearing your favorite band t-shirt. There's attraction toward something that catches our senses. We use conversation starters to meet the other person, from the cliché of "Do you come here often?" to something more original.

You might engage in a longer conversation right there, or exchange contact and decide to grab a coffee or beer another day. The point is that you meet again. While there is a blurry line that separates the attraction from the engagement stage, I generally define the latter as when both parties consciously decide to meet regularly. At this stage, you get to know each other better and learn that you have more in common than just the superficial thing that brought you together. You laugh at the same jokes and share a similar vision for the future.

One day, you might decide to stay together. You might move into the same house, travel the world, start a business or a social impact project together. That's commitment. And unlike many people's perception, you are not done building a relationship once you get there. This stage requires just as much work as all the previous ones and you must continue to engage with them, start conversations and get to know each other better, for as long as you are together. The goal here is to keep it up. Never take anyone's commitment to you for granted. You must continue to host conversations and create encounters that keep the fire up, always reminding you why you stay together.

Stage	Attract	Engage	Stay
Metaphor	**Lighthouse** People are attracted to it, yet don't know what they will find. They are still foreigners at this point.	**Port** People start coming back to it, interacting with various attractions. They start to see familiar faces and feel part of it.	**City** People come back to stay. They choose to commit, be part of it, and build a home there to help develop it further.
Driver	Curiosity	Affinity	Identity
Gathering Icon	Festival: a flagship event that attracts a diverse crowd.	Klatch: a casual gathering focused on conversations.	Dinner: a cozy gathering where people get close and talk intimately.
Example of Action	Create casual, natural, and easy conversation starters. These could be by design (like chatting over the watercooler).	Create reasons for people to return and meet again. Share an events calendar, invite past guests to your next event.	Create roles in the core team, give them more ownership and responsibility for growing your community.

Notes:

- This is a funnel. Not everyone you attract will stay, and not everyone you engage will commit.

- It's not mandatory to follow all steps. Some people will join straight from the engage phase, when they are invited by someone from your community. This is likely if they are already hardcore about the cause, problem, or impact you are focused on.

- The only goal of attracting is to engage, and the only goal of engaging is to commit. Every phase must be continuous over time. You never stop creating activities to attract people. After attracting them, you must create engagement activity, and once they are engaged, you must keep it up to get them committed.

Create a series of MEALs with your "why" embedded into the invitation.

At first, your goal is to be a lighthouse for your community members. For example, Greenpeace is a lighthouse for people who want to save the planet for future generations. Not everyone in the attraction stage truly belongs to you community, but this is the first step to attracting a wider crowd.

The attraction stage serves as a strong tool to embed diversity within the community by reaching out to people beyond your networks to purposefully break your own social bubbles. It is important to be radically inclusive (one of Burning Man's core values). This is a fundamental step to breaking down walls and building bridges. It might even be a good move to put together a crazy MEAL that wildy diversifies the profile of your crowd. Some people attracted to your community might never return. For the number of people who decide to engage, it will be worth it.

As discussed earlier, at the attraction stage I also advise you to find existing places, people, and products that relate to your core. Get to know your crowd and understand what they like and what they feel is missing. Along the way, you will meet people who you share a strong affinity with. Some of these people will also commit as partners, helping to spread your core and grow your community.

Most importantly, lighthouse-stage MEALs only make sense if you also have a strategy to engage people. Most brands do well at attracting people, but not at engaging with them. Cadence is needed to attract, engage, and get them to stay committed to your brand.

When you create a series of activities that deepen your relationship with people, you create more intimate spaces for them to show up authentically over conversation and collaboration.

As you grow from attraction through engagement toward commitment, you build closeness.

CHAPTER 16

Engineering Serendipity: Collision Theory for People

"Great things are done by a series of small things brought together."

—VINCENT VAN GOGH

Enhancing the Probability of Successful Encounters

Engineering serendipity is to enhance the chance of successful encounters by increasing the rate of collisions between people. It's like collision theory applied to humans.

$$\underset{A}{\overset{x}{\underset{x}{\times}}} + \underset{B}{\overset{O}{O}} + \underset{C}{\overset{\triangle\triangle}{\triangleleft}} \longrightarrow \overset{\triangle\triangle}{\underset{\times\times}{\triangle}} \quad OO \;=\; \underset{AC}{\overset{\triangle}{\times}} + \underset{BA}{\overset{O}{\times}} + \underset{CB}{\overset{\triangle}{O}{\triangleleft}}$$

It's about architecting spaces and circumstances that favour collisions between people who otherwise would probably never bump into each other. It is also about engineering diversity by breaking down walls and building bridges. We must purposely design communities that welcome diversity.

Through mixing crowds, we increase serendipitous encounters that spark creativity, which can in turn render positive financial results. "Why Diversity Matters," a 2015 McKinsey study, reports that companies in the top quartile for diversity perform better than the rest. Racial and ethnic diversity can lead to thirty-five percent financial returns above the national average, while gender diversity leads to fifteen percent. Another study by Startup Genome shows that twenty percent of the world's top tech founders are immigrants, while this group represents only four percent of the world's population.

Only through diversity are we able to create something new from scratch. We can't expect a series of unexpectedly positive outcomes from conversations when only discussing the same topics, with the same people, with the same thinking.

Steve Jobs reportedly believed creativity is a result of serendipity. Walter Isaacson, his biographer, quotes Steve Jobs as saying that "Creativity comes from spontaneous meetings, from random discussions. You run into someone, you ask what they're doing, you say 'Wow,' and soon you're cooking up all sorts of ideas." The Pixar studios were built for this, with an atrium designed to engineer employees bumping into each other more often, like a massive watercooler.

The goal is to create collisions that otherwise would not happen. While not every collision yields a successful reaction, engineering serendipity is not about controlling connections, but increasing the rate of encounters that could engender it.

The more collisions, the more likely successful reactions are to happen. The more encounters, the more likely serendipitous connections. Key elements to engineering serendipity:

    a. Frequency: keeping a cadence of encounters

    b. Density: design spaces that are conducive to conversations

    c. Catalyst: anything that accelerates connections

Your purpose is to scale your role as a connector. There is a limit to the number of introductions that one person can make on a one-on-one basis—as your community grows, the less you'll be able to put a name to a face and strategically introduce people where you think it makes sense. That's when you throw parties with a purpose. As we've discussed, it is not about the party, but the conversations around the table.

Your role is not to control connections, but to increase the chances of serendipity by encouraging collisions.

To engineer serendipity, manage the variables you can. Let go of the rest.

> ### Collision Theory for People
>
> The rate of chemical reactions is proportional to the number of collisions between reactant molecules. Molecules must collide to react, but not every collision leads to a successful reaction. It depends both on the amount of energy (the minimum is called activation energy) and orientation of the molecule. Concentration matters too. The more molecules in a delineated space, the more likely the collisions.
>
> A greater concentration will accelerate a reaction. In other words, higher concentration leads to a higher reaction rate. Connecting the metaphor to communities, not every encounter will lead to a serendipitous one, but the more encounters, the more likely it becomes.

Increasing Serendipity Rates

> *"Sitting quietly, doing nothing, Spring comes, and the grass grows, by itself."*
>
> —MATSUO BASHŌ

Your goal is to enhance the probability that serendipitous encounters occur, by increasing the rate of collisions between people.

You can't control the outcome (connections), but you can manage variables that might lead to it:

Frequency

Variable: **Time**

Cadence is fundamental. How regularly do people bump into each other? There is no relationship building without consistent encounters. Trust is built over time. Connecting people through recurring encounters builds familiarity and accelerates the process of belonging.

As seen in the previous chapter, there are different types of events, content or activities to attract people at different levels of awareness, with different purposes. You must design MEALs (aka excuses to bring people together) for multiple purposes (attract, engage or get them to commit) at a specific pace. The pace is to be defined depending on the type of MEAL you are hosting (physical or virtual events, digital content or physical space, etc).

Note on Diversity: for unexpected collisions to occur, you need to purposely attract a diverse group of people and build trust over time. Carefully design your attraction and engagement strategy to mix crowds that belong together, but do not know it yet.

Density

Variable: **Space**

Build closeness and intimacy through space, whether it's physical or virtual. The essence of community is that it is not a monologue, but a multi-directional conversation where all the dots are connected between each other. You want to optimize every bit of space for collisions. There is an optimal ratio to the number of people you would bring together for different purposes. We wouldn't want to host a party for fifteen people in a football stadium.

Regardless of how many people are in, creating a conducive setting is crucial: one where people feel at home to connect. How many people can you fit comfortably in a room? What makes them feel comfortable in this space? If it's a physical space, go for homey seats, warm lighting and temperature. If in a virtual space, help them navigate it with ease. How can you provide a cozy experience where they feel seen, heard and cared for.

Catalyst

Variable: **Trust (or relevance)**

A catalyst increases the rate of reactions. It sparks those seemingly spontaneous connections. When we meet someone who feels familiar, we bond faster than usual. Consciously or not, it stems from perceived trust, provided by relevance. Relevance refers to "preestablished trust" derived from commonalities: a friend in common, a shared music taste, having gone to the same university, etc.

Relevance enhances our predisposition to connect with others.
It can be defined by:

    a. Curation: invite only (or selection process involved)

    b. Seniority: selected people who've achieved something above average

    c. Familiarity: knowing to have something in common, be it a friend or an interest.

People who play a connector role within your community could also be considered catalysts.

In short, a high-relevance context = a higher probability of connection.

> **The Actual Meaning of Serendipity**
>
> The word serendipity comes from a Persian fairy tale about the three princes of Serendib—the ancient name for today's Sri Lanka—who leave the comfort of their palace to travel the world, exploring places and making impressive discoveries along the way.
>
> While there's a magical aura around the world "serendipity," today, there is a hint of detective fiction to the original tale: the princes befriend a nobleman thanks to their abilities to unveil the mystery behind the disappearance of a camel. At its core, the skills that give the three princes their "serendipitous abilities" are rather scientific, based on observation and cleverness.
>
> The key to such "serendipitous discoveries" in their journey isn't fortuitous, but due to intentional observation. The princes are not merely lucky. They are actively observing their surroundings, taking insights from experience to draw conclusions and make decisions.

Serendipitous events are the result of both a curious and attentive state of mind, that integrates previous experiences and learnings into the present. To engineer serendipitous encounters, you must prepare your community to be in the "serendipity mindset." It means to be grateful where you are (abundance), while remaining open and wide awake to opportunities (curious).

ABUNDANCE + CURIOSITY = SERENDIPITY

For magic to happen, you must set the tone. Create environments where people are both at ease and attentive to new opportunities: ready to welcome unexpected outcomes.

Purposefully Mixing People

Whereas traditional marketing aims to lead individuals to take a specific action (make a purchase, sign up for a newsletter, etc), community building is about bringing people together beyond the action they are taking. In other words, the main purpose is beyond the product or service you are providing: value is provided from people to people.

While you might initially attract people around something specific—be it a cause or a product—the ultimate goal is to get people connected.

Still, there is a lot we can learn from well-executed marketing and advertising in order to attract and engage people.

Eugene Schwartz, a marketing expert and the author of *Breakthrough Advertising*, established the importance of customer awareness. He devised a formula with five distinct customer stages:

1. Unaware: doesn't know they have a problem; the hardest to catch (not your focus).

2. Problem/pain aware: knows they have a problem, but doesn't know solutions to it.

3. Solution aware: knows there are solutions, but hasn't chosen one.

4. Product aware: knows about your product, but isn't totally sure about it.

5. Most aware: knows a lot about your product and is likely interested.

Communities start and grow through people at different levels of awareness. Some are knee-deep into your core mission, while others are merely curious. Attracting and engaging all of them is a means to the end: to get people to mix, mingle and influence each other. As a community builder, you must not be the only one speaking: you grow and spread culture faster by bringing the "most aware" ones to influence the most "problem aware."

For the purpose of this book, let's ignore the "unaware" group. These folks are hard to catch, even in traditional advertising.

I'll divide the other levels of awareness in just two: the curious ("solution aware" to "problem aware") and the hardcore ("product aware" to "most aware"). The hardcore are generally the influencers, while the curious are the masses who you would like to influence.

For example, say our goal is to create an entrepreneurial mindset by bringing in founders and seasoned entrepreneurs (the hardcores) to influence a society where fear of failure prevails (by influencing the ones willing to change, but unaware of how: the curious). In another case, we could be trying to encourage a culture of abundance in a context of scarcity (by highlighting the behavior of collaborative people). For a final example, it serves to foster a culture of excellence in a company where most employees are in it for the paycheck.

If you just focus on the hardcore, you likely get a niche, small crowd. You're also at risk of it turning into a Cool Kids Club where many feel excluded, or that they need to be something other than authentic in order to belong.

If you only focus on the curious, you'll grow fast, but miss out on the people who could really help you drive change.

Let's focus on the first example, fostering an entrepreneurial culture in the city. On one side, there are some seasoned founders, people working at startups, and others who just took the leap to start a business (the hardcore). On the other side, there is a crowd of aspiring founders, corporate employees, students and executives (the curious) who may or may not become entrepreneurs and who could learn a lot from the hardcore.

The people in the second group must be brought together with the ones in the first group, in order to create a new mindset in the city. But the people in the first group tend to prefer sharing knowledge with others like them, where they find more concrete value exchange.

How can we mix these crowds? By making friends with each group first. By bringing them together in different instances and building trust to each of them first before then mixing crowds.

Four Steps to Serendipity

The aim is to get the hardcore and the curious groups interacting in one room. To do so, design invitations that cater to different crowds on a consistent timeline: create a series of MEALs that appeal to different crowds.

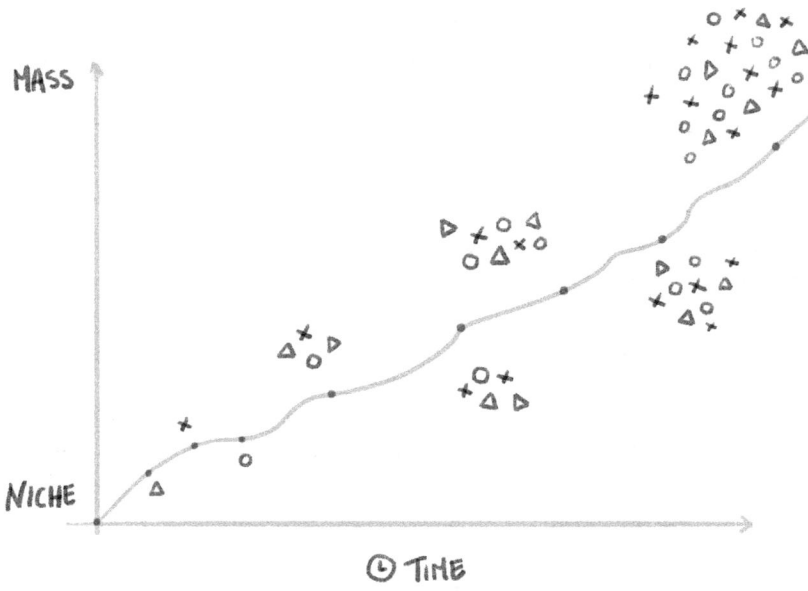

Step One: Get Yourself Together

In the previous chapters, you've defined your core, crafted a story, and brainstormed ways to attract and engage people and to get them committed. These previous steps are fundamental in order to proceed with the next ones.

Step Two: Engage the Hardcore

The hardcore are the people who are most committed and engaged within your community. For example, in the yoga community, these would be the teachers. In a startup ecosystem, they would be the seasoned founders or highly skilled developers.

Hardcore members may join you straight from the engagement stage; since they already share your core, they "get it" faster. They're either most aware about what you offer, or they know a lot about a specific topic or interest related to your core. Still, attraction-stage activities might bring some hardcore people who are outside your social bubbles. To engage the hardcore, figure out how you add value for them. This is important because these people can add a ton of value to your community. Make sure they are interested in your project and feel appreciated. Examples include inviting them to founders-only private dinners or inviting them to speak and share their thoughts.

Step Three: Start Catering for a Wider Crowd (Keeping the Hardcore Engaged)

Expand your focus to people who are curious, but not yet deep into your core.

To attract them, keep the invitation simple. For example, invite a few popular entrepreneurs to join a panel or fireside chat, or host meetups with special guests who they might be familiar with. Gathering around food tends to be a popular solution across the world.

Before they leave, give them reason to come back. Invite them to stay in touch, inform them of the next event, make them more aware about how they can engage with you onwards.

Step Four: Keep Cadence And Start Mixing Crowds

By winning people's trust and sharing your core, you are likely building a bond that goes beyond *what* the invitation is about.

Eventually, people will join your events because they trust who is inviting them: you (personally, or as in your brand). The people who accepted your previous invitations might now be willing to join any future events you host. At this stage, you have the opportunity to create varied content that brings different crowds together. From here, you can become a platform for diverse worlds to collide.

For example:

    a. Invite some of the hardcore as speakers or co-hosts at events targeted to the curious crowd. It's a win-win from every angle.

    b. Host a larger event targeting the hardcore, and make room to invite the most engaged people from the curious crowd.

    c. Create a new MEAL to bring everyone together, centered around something that caters to everyone.

    d. Repeat.

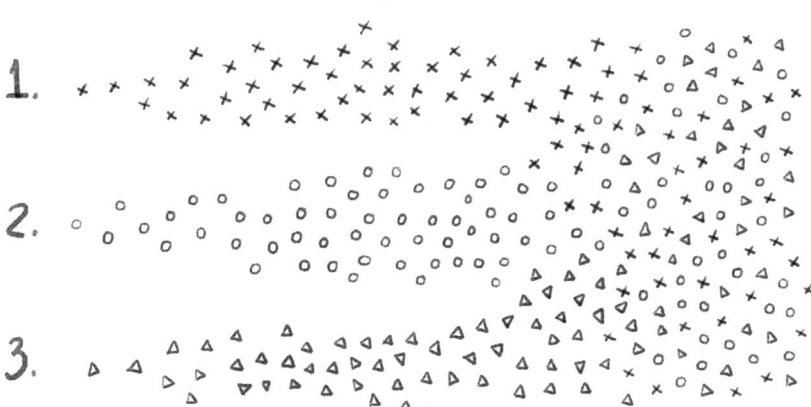

For as long as your community lives, you must continue to attract, engage, and commit with people. Follow the three Cs, honor your core, and grow trust.

> **Note:** Categorizing people as "hardcore" or "curious" is inspired by Schwartz's levels of awareness, and can apply to different circles of people. Community can be based on interests (beer and wine lovers), demographics (senior and youth), or backgrounds. So you could connect hardcore or curious people from very different backgrounds if they are engaged in the same topic. For example, bringing together techies (developers, coders), artists (painters, designers), academics (teachers, researchers) and business people (sales, marketing, operations) to brainstorm long-term solutions to diversity or climate change.

Memorable Moments: Encounters that Can Spark Serendipity

As you know by now, *what* brings us together is just as important as how we get together. Memorable moments are unique experiences that become stories owned by the people within your community. Having such experiences enhances their sense of belonging while they organically spread the word about your community.

According to renowned Malaysia-based placemaking expert NanI Kahar, people make a place their own when they create memories around it—when they have stories to tell around that bench, under that tree, or on that street, it feels like that is their place. When people make good memories, they make it theirs. It creates ownership and they tell stories about it.

Here are a couple of ways you can design spaces that create serendipity and inspire stories that will be shared through your community.

The Watercooler Effect

Create "landmarks" that serve as conversation starters, and make the space purposefully inconvenient.

According to biographer Walter Isaacson, Steve Jobs had the Pixar building designed to promote encounters and unplanned collaborations "...to make people get out of their offices and mingle in the central atrium with people they might not otherwise see." Renowned Pixar animator John Lasseter said that the space "would draw you to the center, or have you crossing it, many times a day." It worked. He shares, "I kept running into people I hadn't seen for months. I've never seen a building that promoted collaboration and creativity as well as this one."

Feels Like Home

Keep it casual. Make it feel like home.

Choose warm lights over cool white. Dimmed over bright. Cushioned over hard chairs. Couches over chairs, if you can afford them. Offer some snacks that are easy to eat while talking, accompanied by a warm drink on a cozy couch or something chilled on a summer terrace. Keep close together, rather than spread out. If dining, set up one long table, like a big Italian family.

For a group sharing or discussion, set up everyone in a circle. If someone is delivering a workshop or a presentation, arrange the audience in a semi-circle around them. I'd only pick a classroom setup such as an auditorium if you're holding knowledge-sharing sessions with experts from your community. If you do use a lecture hall or auditorium, keep it to a maximum of five rows, with extra room at the side where people can share drinks or snacks before and after the talk. Choose a cocktail setup, where people stand and roam freely, maybe with a few islands of tables and chairs where they can sit and talk for a bit longer. Make sure to keep the space tight with people close to each other in every circumstance.

Setup examples:

- Long table: family feeling
- Semi-circle: facilitated conversation, workshop
- Circle: distributed conversation, group sharing
- Small auditorium: knowledge sharing, fireside chat (Pecha Kucha, Startup Grind)
- Cocktail: organic conversations, standing and free to roam

Note: If you are hosting a virtual space, carefully pick your words, palette, images, and fonts to make it inviting. The style may differ depending on the platform you're using. Opt for platforms that are forum-like (Reddit or Facebook groups) or chat-like (Slack, mIRC, WhatsApp), over platforms that feel like a monologue (like a static website). As tech evolves, this is an ongoing conversation.

Serendipity Dinners

It was May 2014. I had been living in Malaysia for three months and was preparing to host the first of what would become a series of private dinners to connect foreign VCs with local founders and community builders.

The idea came from talking with Vinnie Lauria, founding partner of Golden Gate Ventures, a Singapore-based VC. I met Vinnie during a break at a private conference held at the Microsoft office in Singapore. He gave me a fifteen-minute mentoring session on the need to foster interactions and natural conversations among founders and investors within the Malaysian startup ecosystem. There were international folks who were interested to learn more about Malaysia, and I was willing to help connect the local startup ecosystem with that of greater Southeast Asia.

Vinnie suggested I host a casual dinner with "no agenda, no speed dating, no activities. Just bring people together around some food and drinks and let them talk."

I liked the thought, but hadn't hosted an event with such a loose agenda before. So I did and called it Serendipity Dinner. I invited a fair representation of the Malaysian startup ecosystem to one restaurant. There were around eighteen founders, ten key community leaders, three local investors, and five government representatives. It even included the CEOs of Malaysia's largest public fund, Cradle Fund, and of its most relevant agencies, MDeC, as well as the Malaysian Global Innovation and Creativity Centre. The event turned out larger than planned—I advise fifteen to eighteen people for cozy dinners—but it was a great success. Conversation flowed, and the only interruption was the toast. I introduced the host, who said a few words, reminded people of their purpose there, and then let the conversation continue.

I met people who would go on to become my best friends and biggest supporters as an entrepreneur and community builder in Malaysia. Kristine Lauria would become a fellow community builder, informal mentor, and partner at The List KL, which eventually became the most popular weekly newsletter for events in tech, design, and business in Kuala Lumpur. Another founder, Francesca Chia, became a lifelong friend and she also met future mentors and investors at this dinner. The connections from that night rippled over time. Its spark started a fire.

I continued hosting Serendipity Dinners. Each was hosted by international investors from a different country and held at a different location, always with unexpected and unforgettable experiences for its participants.

The success of Serendipity Dinners was seventy-five percent from the people invited and twenty-five percent from there being a memorable setting and no agenda. My favorite dinner was held at a large converted warehouse in an old historical printing factory, with the scent of ink in the air and fairy lights strung from the ceiling. We hired a popular grassroots mixologist to create a pop-up gin bar, and served finger foods. We invited a selection of Malaysian founders to eat, drink, and share. The rest was pure magic.

A high rate of serendipitous encounters reflects high relevance within your community. By enhancing it, you can create a series of memorable moments to generate incredible stories that will be shared by your members.

Gathering consistently is key to building trust. Allow people to interact often and get to know each other. By enhancing the incidence of familiar faces in the room, you can make people feel at home.

To enhance the probability of serendipity, people need to feel relevance in the context. They must share one thing in common: the core.

In bringing different minds to collide consistently enough, people discover the ways in which they relate, whether it's their purpose, value systems, or beliefs. You end up connecting dots that originally seemed disconnected.

CHAPTER 17

From Seed Head to Flying: Closeness Circles

"The best way to find out if you can trust somebody is to trust them."

—ERNEST HEMINGWAY

Core, Communication, Cadence

The more you grow, the more you make space for new roles within your community.

Those who feel the most at home in your community will grow a sense of ownership towards it, and might become committed to help it grow. In feeling ownership, they will develop a natural sense of ambassadorship. The most committed members of your community will walk closer to your core, as if stepping into your inner circle. As these relationships deepen, you will grow closer to them. Closeness brings in more intimate conversations, which implies trust.

There are certain things you share with your closest friends that you wouldn't share through social media. The same for news that you share first with your family. The closer you get, the more you commit.

Trust is both built and maintained by authentic communication. The more you grow familiar with someone, the more likely it is that you communicate authentically with them. Similarly, the more authentically you communicate with people and they perceive your vulnerability, the more they become aware of their privilege in being trusted, and the more likely that it strengthens the bond between you. In an ideal scenario, trust grows in both directions.

It is your responsibility as a community builder to create communication systems that build and maintain trust, while providing tools to empower people to help your community grow.

The Closeness Circles

The closer you get to someone, the deeper your conversation becomes.

This concentric circles framework illustrates a communication system with different levels of interaction. The layers define the cadence (frequency) and depth (intimacy) of communication between you and other people within your community.

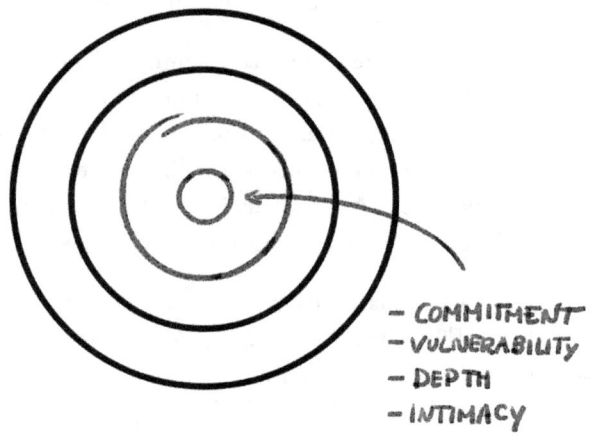

Its purpose is not to place people in bubbles, but to help you organize your communication, creating a system that:

1. Strengthens bonds with those you're closer with;

2. Helps newcomers to step closer to your core at their own pace.

A well designed communication system allows people in the outer layers to get to know you better, while growing into a closer level of trust. It also helps you to strengthen trust with those in the innermost layers, until they are so close to the core of your community that they become its key representatives: people will help you grow.

Getting Closer

It is natural that your closest friends are people who you've known for a long time, or the ones who have been with you through ups and downs. They might be people you've known since childhood, with whom you spent a lot of time, or shared intense experiences with.

It is also normal to build faster ties with a friend of a friend through inherited trust.

While you are likely to grow closer to people who have been in your community for a longer period of time, there are different variables that matter to building closeness. The frequency of encounters between people, as well as their level of engagement with others within your community, highly influences how close they get to your core, over time.

One of the most common ways of moving deeper into the core of the Closeness Circles is through wholehearted (genuine) contribution. Regardless of how long a person has been in your community, some people become intimate at a faster pace by adding value first. People who are intrinsically aligned with the idea of "giving before taking" (abundance), who comprehend that "we rise by lifting others" (humility), and act accordingly to these ideas with sincerity, from their hearts (authenticity). In doing so, they naturally act in accordance with the community's core values (abundance, humility, authenticity), and might grow closer to its core, faster.

The closer to your inner circles, the more essential is their role in the community.

While people at the very core of your community become a key part of it, it is important to note that walking into your inner circle should not resemble joining a Cook Kids Club.

The ones closest to the core not only get insider benefits or privileged information, but also more responsibilities. They are required to act towards the common good and represent the community, making sure their actions and words reflect its core. They are committed to giving.

In absolute: people closer to the core and inner circle should not only be "like-minded-peeps" who do all they can to please you and think themselves more special than the rest. Diversity ensures representation, which means simply that a wider range of ways of thinking and feeling are covered. Statistically speaking, diversity also speaks good things of you and other leaders within your community: that you're welcoming people based on shared values represented by actions, not by what they look like.

Being closer to the inner circles of a community doesn't mean a reward, although it is a position of honor. It is a place reached by those who decided to give more, work harder, and help others more frequently. Ironically, it is the place for those who worked to make more space for others.

The core of a community belongs to those who have expressed its core values the most.

Exploring Closeness Layers

While the structure of the closeness circles may be clear to someone at the core level, the idea is that it remains undisclosed to those in the outer layers, to avoid creating negative group dynamics where newcomers feel excluded.

The variable in this diagram is vulnerability. The closer to the center, the more vulnerable you are to the people included in it.

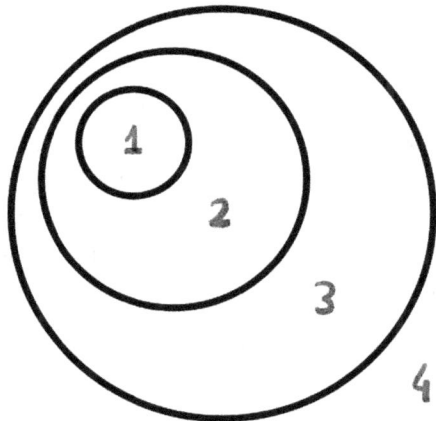

1. Core group

2. Inner circle

3. Network

4. Crowd (beyond the circle, outer layer)

Having layers of communication is natural to humans. Our relationships grow from interactions, creating familiarity and trust. In a nutshell, we can say the variable for closeness is vulnerability.

I chose three levels as a minimum because it helps build and keep balance within a community. When there are only two levels, you can create an inside/outside dynamic with some people boasting or trying to attain power that they do not own, while others may feel excluded, compromising the sense of trust and safety that is fundamental for the community to simply exist. At three levels you lessen the risk of polarity—from there, you can grow into more layers outwards, depending on the complexity of your community.

At the end of this chapter, you'll have enough insights to draw your own Closeness Circles.

The Origins of the Framework

The Closeness Circles framework is inspired by the work of Robin Dunbar, an anthropologist and psychologist whose work gave rise to the idea that a person's personal network could reach no more than 150. This is actually a simplification. What Dunbar actually meant is that our direct group of contact is within a range of one hundred to two hundred people, depending on how social you are. These are the people you'd call for a large party.

There are also different layers to this network. The closest five are the people who are most essential to you, including family members. Next, there are around fifteen people you would call your closest friends. Then, up to fifty are the ones you're likely to invite to a casual party. From fifty to 150 are the rest of your friend group. The groups could also grow beyond 150 to five hundred—your acquaintances—and out to 1,500, representing your broader network.

I developed the closeness circles by thinking of a simplified version of Dunbar's theory. At the very center are your core people. In the outer layer, your inner circle. In the third and outermost layer, your network. These three circles represent your community.

You could draw more layers within your community, but I prefer keeping it simple. I believe these categories are the fundamental ones. You can add layers as they fit for your needs. For example, in a company the circles could comprise:

1. At its core, our team

2. At the second layer, clients and advisory board

3. At its third layer, partners and ambassadors

4. At the fourth, our community (regular readers and subscribers)

5. At its final layer, our broader network

This structure defines how you should communicate with different people within the ecosystem of your own community. It seems unreasonable, even for the most inexperienced of us, to share something with your broader network that has not yet been communicated to your team.

The more inward we dive, the deeper we go within a community. The more aware you are of the happenings, the shortcomings, and the latest news, the more you build closeness. In other words, communication can be used as a tool to build trust and engineer closeness levels within your community.

Most importantly, belonging to these layers must be a transparent and merit-driven process that is based on how much people have given back to the community. It is not a competition. Belonging to the innermost circles should not represent a reward, although it should be an honor to belong there. The most collaborative are likely to get there first. The inner circles should represent the people who have given the most to your community, who worked the hardest giving back to others and who have helped to create a safe space for everyone.

Next Steps

Draft your own inner circle based on the ideas we've explored.

Below, I've shared an example I used with a company I founded back in 2017. Note that it was a consulting business, in which I considered the clients my closest fellows after my team because I wanted them to feel that way.

Whenever good news came, my team would hear about it first, and then they would prepare an appropriate communication to my clients via email. Partners and ambassadors would hear later. Our crowd of loyal subscribers would hear about it through the monthly newsletter. The broader network would find out through public media (news channels and social media). This way, even in the smallest details, our clients felt close to us.

By simply organizing our communication system to include "closeness" as a variable, we were able to engineer belonging and made some key people understand how special they were to us.

This example serves to merely illustrate how your communication strategy (channels, message, frequency) can be conceptualized and organized by the Closeness Circles.

CHAPTER 18

Cultivating Dandelions: Let it Grow

"Fight for the things that you care about, but do it in a way that will invite others to join you."

—RUTH BADER GINSBURG

Your Identity as a Community Builder

In your journey as a community builder, you will grow into different roles at each stage.

While you may start off as the key player bringing people together—including all the development and logistics around physical or virtual spaces—you might end up as the guiding point for others who will play this role after you, expanding your community or growing their own communities. You and your community may become their compass. You go from organizing an event to developing a trust system.

Changing roles within a community means that it is growing.

As a good leader, be open to letting go of past roles with grace. Make space for others to take on these roles, change, innovate and expand around it to grow the whole community.

A quick recap: building communities is about "growing familiarity through a cadence of encounters that spark serendipity" (creating excuses to bring people together consistently enough). Eventually, people will start to find familiar faces in the crowd. Each time they return, they feel more at home. Some people greet each other by name, while others notice newcomers and join you in welcoming them. Create safe spaces where people can show up as their most authentic self. When you live, speak, create, or vibrate according to your own frequency, you attract the right people. When you build a brand from a strong core, everything you say and do resembles you. Connect authentically. Make friends, not contacts. Build relationships, not transactions. Values define decisions, which define actions, which define culture. This includes how people interact with others and react to situations, even when no one is looking.

While community building remains "the art of bringing people together," it doesn't mean that you need to keep playing the same role. As your community grows, it won't be fully managed by you, nor people directly managed by you. It may grow to a point where you've expanded the role of bringing people together to a thousand people. True communities grow like nature does: organically. They require leaders who are brave enough to trust, empower, and let go. Building true communities means constantly daring to make yourself obsolete, by empowering others to take on roles you used to have.

Empowerment is about building (and reinforcing) culture. Paul Graham is co-founder of Y-Combinator, the world's first and top startup accelerator, which is responsible for setting the context of growth for companies like Airbnb, Stripe, and Dropbox. He says, "Culture is important in any organization, but YC culture wasn't just how we behaved when we built the product. At YC, the culture was the product."

Allow people to represent you by empowering them with your voice and message. When you start by attracting people who align with your core, this comes almost naturally.

As a true leader, you must empower people with the core which defines their everyday decisions, actions and behaviors. It gets better if you also share knowledge, tools, tricks and tech to help them spread their voice, spreading your core along with it.

Above all, you must trust them to represent your core. And let go.

Manage what you can. Let go of everything else.

From Builder to Connector: Be the First Dandelion

Recalling what we discussed earlier—that while you might have created the brand, space, and the initial excuses to bring them together, the reason people stay connected belongs to everyone. The core belongs to the community. Be the first dandelion, and let your seeds fly.

As we considered in the previous chapter: the closer they are to your core, the more likely people are to represent your community and help you grow.

But while it is fundamental, it is not enough to just "trust and let them grow." If you don't create a growth infrastructure to help them do so (that includes knowledge sharing, information management, intelligence, platform and tools to facilitate the process), it won't go anywhere.

Because belonging is among the most ancient of our needs, as technology develops, there are a growing number of solutions to help communities grow. One could start, manage, and grow a fully fledged community through existing free tools. Finding the ideal platform depends on the development stage, layers in your Closeness Circles, and overall profile of your community.

One great example of growth infrastructure is that of Startup Grind. When I started there back in 2012, we handled everything using a mix of existing platforms and simple yet customizable web pages. My closest friend, Francisco Cruz, hacked a ton of no-code stuff to make it happen and we had an amazing growth infrastructure that allowed us to grow from twenty to nearly 180 chapters within a couple of years. While Francisco's hacks served us well for a long period of time, around 2014, Startup Grind's founder and CEO envisioned a platform to help local directors grow further and better. It worked. The last time I checked, Startup Grind had over six hundred chapters all over the world, and was still growing. The organization's system evolved into a fully fledged business, Bevy, which currently helps large companies grow their own communities.

While you do not need to create a complex platform to get started, I strongly suggest creating a minimum growth infrastructure that allows others to replicate what you have done. Start with simple manuals and cheat-sheets that serve as a shortcut to success for a first-time community builder. I worked on a few of those in the early days at Startup Grind.

On the technology side, you could start from a combination of group chats (for the core people), online forums (for the most engaged), and a public page (for the newcomers), all complemented by free webinar and online conferencing platforms that help people meet recurrently.

Developing a platform for your community is an important part of accelerating its growth, but it is not required from the outset. First, focus on the human factor: get your core straight, attract and engage people who share your values, and get them committed to help you grow.

But, just as it is not enough to trust and let them grow if you don't create a growth infrastructure to help them in doing so, it is not enough to create a badass infrastructure if you fail at empowering community members. To grow a community, you must empower people with a true sense of belonging and trust.

Dare to make yourself obsolete. As your community grows, you become less of a key player to bring people together and more of a connector. From there, they belong together. It's no longer about you.

FINAL WORDS

There's No Place Like Home

> *"It is good to have an end to journey toward;
> but it is the journey that matters, in the end."*
>
> —ERNEST HEMINGWAY

Coming Home: An Unexpected Journey

This book was first idealized in 2014. I thought of it as an article that I would title "Hacking Communities." In its first draft, the piece outlined how I had come to play a key role in the Malaysian startup ecosystem, after landing in Kuala Lumpur knowing only two people there. Within just six months, I was working with key players in the Southeast Asian tech scene and was a community ambassador for the National Government of Malaysia. I moved there for a one-year experience in a full-time job, but quit within three months and stayed in the country for over four years, building communities and contributing to the development of the startup ecosystem.

I wanted to put on paper how this experience happened, in order to help others navigate communities and ecosystems. But it felt too soon, back then. I decided to keep working and gather more knowledge in the field of community building before sharing that article. I also wanted to validate the impact of my work before putting anything out in the world. In the years that followed, community building became my core activity—it's what I care for and what I do on a daily basis.

I didn't just stay longer in Malaysia than I expected and for unforeseen reasons. I also discovered a career path I hadn't planned: as an entrepreneur and a community builder.

After leaving the company that acquired mine in 2017, I decided to take on that article again, only now, it would be a book. I couldn't fit it all in one article. As I started writing, I went on yet another unexpected journey that led me to visit startup ecosystems and attend conferences around the world, from Malaysia to Alexandria, Madrid, Barcelona, Mexico City, Dubai, and, finally, Lisbon. From this last city, I decided to take a train to Porto and embarked on a three hundred kilometer pilgrimage to Santiago de Compostela. Every step as a pilgrim led me to life-changing decisions. One key decision was that *Hacking Communities* (the book) had to be published in 2018. The other was to leave Malaysia, in order to find a place closer to Brazil (where my whole family still lives) to call home.

I became a nomad again, roaming from Bali, Indonesia, to Norwich, England, and shortly back to Brazil, then to San Francisco. In this book, I write about the loneliness I experienced here. San Francisco taught me a tough lesson about belonging, which led me to rewrite a lot of chapters in this book. It taught me that building communities isn't all about knowing the framework, as much as it is about being in the right state of mind. I, who had grown to identify myself as a good connector and community builder, felt lonely. I felt ashamed. That California time hindered my writing. I got stuck with imposter syndrome. Part of me wishes I had not been through this, but I am aware that experiencing loneliness in one of the most vibrant (and one of my favorite) cities in the world was fundamental to my journey in writing this book. The result is not much of a handguide, but more of a guide to the key principles, values, and mindset that define a community builder.

As much as I couldn't have released this book as an article in 2014, I couldn't have done it in 2018 either. I found that you need more than a framework to build a community—you need to step into your own journey home, towards your most authentic self. My personal journey turned this book into a more spiritual than practical guide to community building. It isn't enough to know what to do. You need to mean it. Because ultimately, building communities is about relationships, not transactions. You need to work on it wholeheartedly, which implies you must be vulnerable. To be vulnerable, you must be courageous. Remember that courage means an act from the heart.

João Guimarães Rosa, one of Brazil's greatest novelists (and a fellow countryman of Minas Gerais), says, "Life is like this: it heats up and cools down, it squeezes and then loosens, it becomes calm and the restless. What it wants from us is courage." I returned "home" to the countryside of Brazil after ten years away in 2020. At the time, the whole world faced one of the biggest crises of our era: the COVID-19 pandemic. In the same year, I wrote the following words in an article featured on *Badass Times*: "I never thought of myself as an entrepreneur. Dad is a farmer, mom is a banker (for real). I'm glad the community around me inspired me to follow the ugly duckling path. I probably wouldn't have had the idea of the company I started, had I not been surrounded by founders, companies, digital nomads, and other people whose problem I would solve."

I had never heard the term "community building" before 2014, even though it describes what I had been working on since 2007. Communities helped me find my true home. I learned that context matters: sharing space and time with people who leveled me up and inspired me to be my most authentic self made a big impact. Ultimately, I found that a true sense of home is found nowhere geographically, but in three places:

- Within us
- Among others (community)
- On the way

Becoming a Community Builder: On the Way

All the steps I've described led me here, finishing this book from a farm, back in Brazil. Isn't it ironic? There and back again, like Bilbo Baggins. Coming back, I found that belonging is a big deal to me, not because I'm great at it, but because I struggle with it.

The Cowardly Lion struggles with the courage he thinks he lacks. He aims to find his courage, joining Dorothy on the Yellow Brick Road towards the Great Wizard of Oz (who would grant his desires). But the lion is unaware that, on the way, he is demonstrating that he is the most courageous of all his fellows, through small acts. Often, we are already that which we aim to become in our hearts, but it's in the journey that we develop the strength, habits, and skills to become fully ourselves.

My own journey as an entrepreneur and community builder is that of an ugly duckling. I left my small town when I was a kid, to go to a larger one where I'd be more exposed to different people and opportunities. At a very young age, I discovered the importance of surroundings in helping us become who we are, for good or bad. We might become the most authentic version of ourselves, or struggle to fit in. At the age of eighteen, I moved alone into a big city, and reinvented myself. At twenty, I left Brazil and did not come back until I was thirty. Throughout that journey, I had the luck to deconstruct myself completely, a necessary step in rebuilding myself. I moved to places where I did not belong and found ways to connect with others unlike me. I found ways to make friends with strangers. Throughout my journey, I struggled with belonging. But it is the need for connection that led me to build communities.

Step Your Foot Out of the Door

I still remember reaching the iconic Santiago de Compostela Cathedral, which marks the end of the pilgrimage. I felt unsettled and with a sense of peace and emptiness, all at once. I noticed that what mattered wasn't the destination, but the path itself. As Hemingway said, "It is the journey that matters, in the end." It is the journey that makes the hero. The story develops the character. It is the process of building a community that makes you a community builder. What you need to get started is already within: we all care to belong. We all struggle with it.

As I discussed in the introduction to this book, our first step is to recognize and cultivate a sense of home. We can do this little by little. Being yourself, or better put, becoming yourself, is a journey, not a destination. Community is about sharing your home with others. It's not about you alone, but about the people you would like to host. First, step into your inner home. Then, be courageous enough to share it with others.

The rest is your story.

ACKNOWLEDGMENTS

This book would not have been possible without people who showed up on my path and shared a bit of their journey with me.

The beauty of the organic connections enabled by communities is that one single gesture can spark a series of events that change someone's life. Every dot in the network matters. Every person we meet can spark a positive chain reaction. I recognize that one small action led to the events that have helped to define who I am. I am a result of all the people I met on my path. My time in Malaysia caused me to bloom as a community builder, but what got me there matters.

Through working for a nonprofit, I became connected to Marina Ponzi, who introduced me to Marta Cruz, co-founder of NXTP Labs, one of Latin America's first startup accelerators. These two facilitated my first experiences in building startup communities. Marina was a role model for my career, even before I knew that what we both did was called community building. Marta was an invaluable resource and reference point in entrepreneurship and leadership. As a result of joining NXTP Labs, I became Startup Grind's Buenos Aires Director.

Thanks to Startup Grind, I started building communities in Kuala Lumpur as soon as I landed. Derek Andersen, its founder, trusted me to grow this community across Africa and Asia-Pacific, and I met people who would become life-long friends, mentors, and partners across Southeast Asia (and the world, I'd say). Derek also gave me the keystone of what would become the core values and the first framework of community building, which I developed to write this book. He phrased the value of abundance as "give first," and that of authenticity as "make friends, not contacts." To this day, he is an inspiration and an example of a true community builder.

ACKNOWLEDGMENTS

What happened after I landed in Malaysia was a series of serendipitous events that led me to be at my best, and I have many people to thank.

First, my fellow community builders across Southeast Asia, who shared with me the passion needed to make various startup ecosystems grow. These people taught me the meaning of true collaboration. Thanks to Dash Dakshinamoorthy, Bowel Gai, and Daniel Cerventus, who helped me to make connections with the people and projects that led to me taking on a key role in the region. Thank you to Cheryl Yeoh, Grace Sai, Amarit Charoenphan, Steve Munroe, Vinnie, and Kristine Lauria, who got me involved in life-changing projects and helped me to make authentic connections along the way. Thanks also to Lalitha Wemel, Oko Davaasuren, Feng Lim, Heislyc Loh, Curry Khoo, Marcus Foon, Maverick Foo, Zikry Kholil, Arzumy MD, and their teams, who helped me feel that I was not alone building communities and that sharing the journey with friends made it better. These people have a place in my heart and remain my favorite crew of community builders.

Hacking Communities is a result of my experiences in various communities, but most of it derives from startup communities and they inspired most of the examples in this book. My experience building and researching these communities dictates most of my beliefs around what brings and keeps people together. Yet other communities inspired my most original thoughts, for true creativity that can only emerge from diverse minds getting together. Thanks to JF Gauthier and Marc Penzel, the co-founders of Startup Genome, I developed the frameworks in this book through evidence-based, research-driven insights. They also helped me make connections with creative and artistic communities beyond startups, from San Francisco to Berlin.

ACKNOWLEDGMENTS

I would like to thank my closest ones: my friends and family. Having natural community builders among my closest friends (and roommates) has improved everything I do on a daily basis. Thanks to Jaclyn Lee, who led conscious-fashion and plant-based communities in Malaysia. Thanks to Natasha Zolotareva, who stood at the head of Kuala Lumpur's Creative Mornings, and to Cynthia Wong, who brought the entire yoga community of Malaysia together through amazing events and retreats. Thank you also to Erum Azeez, who managed Project Renaissance and is a natural center of gravity for nerds and founders.

Last, but not least, I would like to thank my father, mother, brother, and sister-in law, who supported me unconditionally throughout my journey, always helping me to remember where I came from. Deep inside I am still a kid from a small town in Brazil who spent holidays with a very large extended family. A part of me still misses my grandparents' home with the long table, around which more than fifty people would squeeze in to pray, dine, and laugh together. At my grandma's, we were not rich, but we were abundant: there would always be more than enough food and room for one more. As I traveled the world, a part of me struggled to find the same sense of home I got at those messy evenings at my grandma's. A part of me is still replicating her best practices out in the world. She understood that family is where your heart is.

This book is dedicated to everyone who loves their families and wants to create a sense of home for others: no matter who they are or where they came from. Thank you for reading this.

I wish you a worthwhile journey!

Laís

THINGS TO READ AND WATCH

Brown, Brené, *Braving the Wilderness: The Quest for True Belonging and the Courage to Stand Alone.*

Brown, Brené, *Daring Greatly: How the Courage to Be Vulnerable Transforms the Way We Live, Love, Parent, and Lead.*

Brown, Brené, *The Gifts of Imperfection: Let Go of Who You Think You're Supposed to Be and Embrace Who You Are.*

Cacioppo, John T. and Patrick, William, *Loneliness: Human Nature and the Need for Social Connection.*

Cacioppo, John T., Stephanie Cacioppo, John P. Capitanio, and Steven W. Cole, "**The Neuroendocrinology of Social Isolation.**"

Campbell, Joseph, *The Hero with a Thousand Faces.*

de Oliveira, Laís, "**The ugly duckling road to badass entrepreneurship,**" *Badass Times*, October 22, 2020.

Endeavor Global, "**The Multiplier Effect: How a Network of Entrepreneurs Created a Tech Sector in Argentina,**" Feb 10, 2012.

Esperón, Augustín. "**Startup accelerators helped spark Latin America's tech boom,**" *Tech Crunch*, October 4, 2018.

THINGS TO READ AND WATCH

Feld, Brad and Ian Hathaway, *Startup Communities: Building an Entrepreneurial Ecosystem in Your City.*

Feld, Brad and Ian Hathaway, *The Startup Community Way: Evolving an Entrepreneurial Ecosystem.*

Harari, Yuval Noah, *Sapiens: A Brief History of Humankind.*

Harari, Yuval Noah. "**What Explains the Rise of Humans?**" TEDGlobalLondon, June 2015.

Hunt, Vivian, Dennis Layton, and Sara Prince, "**Why Diversity Matters,**" McKinsey & Company.

Kahneman, Daniel, *Thinking, Fast and Slow.*

Khazan, Olga. "**How Loneliness Begets Loneliness,**" *The Atlantic*, April 6, 2017.

Laing, Olivia, *The Lonely City: Adventures in the Art of Being Alone.*

Mander, Benedict, "**Argentina: home to the majority of Latin America's tech unicorns,**" *Financial Times*, September 19, 2016.

Morelix, Arnobio, "The Heroes of America's Startup Economy Weren't Born in America," *Inc.*

Pinker, Susan, "The secret to living longer may be your social life," TED2017, April 2017.

Pinker, Susan, *The Village Effect: How Face-to-Face Contact Can Make Us Healthier, Happier, and Smarter.*

Pinkola Estés, Clarissa, *Women Who Run with the Wolves: Myths and Stories of the Wild Woman Archetype.*

Ray, Tiernan, "Steve Jobs said Silicon Valley needs serendipity, but is it even possible in a Zoom world?" ZDNet.

Sinek, Simon, "How great leaders inspire action," TEDxPuget Sound, September 2009.

For more recommendations, see
hackingcommunities.com/read-this

ABOUT THE AUTHOR

An entrepreneur with over a decade of experience in community building, **Laís de Oliveira** has participated in the development of entrepreneurial communities around the world.

From Minas Gerais, Brazil, she moved to Mauritius in 2010 to work as a volunteer with nonprofit organization AIESEC. From there, she went on to manage eighteen chapters and almost two thousand volunteers at the same organization, across Argentina, Chile, and Uruguay.

After leaving AIESEC, Laís stayed in Argentina and joined one of Latin America's first startup accelerators. She also joined Startup Grind as their Buenos Aires Director and joined an edtech startup to organize the first online startup conference in Latin America.

ABOUT THE AUTHOR

In 2014, she moved to Malaysia and created Startup Grind in Kuala Lumpur. She also joined the headquarters of the Startup Grind community as Africa and APAC Community Director, contributing to the growth of more than eighty chapters. At the same time, she joined an initiative by the Malaysian Government as a community ambassador, with an aim to develop the country's startup ecosystem. From there, she helped develop Malaysia's largest educational initiative for entrepreneurship, MaGIC Academy, and served both as a community consultant and as a Mentor in Residence at Southeast Asia's largest startup accelerator, the Global Accelerator Program.

During her time in Malaysia, Laís also started her first business, 8spaces.co. A marketplace for flexible commercial real estate, its clients included Heineken, GSK, Google, Swarovski, and Etsy. In 2016, it was acquired by Flyspaces.com, Southeast Asia's largest marketplace for workspaces. After acquisition, Laís served as Malaysia Country Manager and Chief Community Officer.

She then moved to San Francisco, where she joined Startup Genome as the organization's Community Development Director. There, she developed evidence-based strategies to accelerate economic growth through startup communities and worked for governments and innovation agencies in more than seventy-five ecosystems as part of the executive team.

In 2020, Laís moved back to Brazil. With friends, she is building a rural office in Serra do Cipó national park while considering her next steps. She joined the On Deck Fellowship in October 2020 and is currently developing companies focused on the future of living, of work, and of education.

NOTES

www.ingramcontent.com/pod-product-compliance
Lightning Source LLC
Chambersburg PA
CBHW060830220526
45466CB00003B/1042